George A. Romero

George A. Romero

Tom Fallows and Curtis Owen

www.pocketessentials.com

For Art Higham, Rob Talbot & Verica Travar
They taught us everything we know. . . so blame them

First published in 2008 by Pocket Essentials
P.O. Box 394, Harpenden, Herts, AL5 1XJ
www.pocketessentials.com

A CIP catalogue record for this book is available from the British Library.

ISBN 978-1-84243-282-2

2 4 6 8 10 9 7 5 3 1

Typeset by Ellipsis Books Limited, Glasgow
Printed and bound in Great Britain by CPI Cox and Wyman, Reading

'They're coming to get you, Barbra!'
Johnny, *Night of the Living Dead* (1968)

Tom would like to thank…

Darren Horne, Emily Williams, Stuart Green at ForeeFest,
Ed Lawrenson, Hannah Bayley, Hannah at Pocket Essentials,
David Pickerill, Ben & Jay, Tom Atkins and Mum and John
for putting up with me and putting me up

Curtis would like to thank…

My parents for letting me watch horror films as a kid, my
Nan and Granddad, thanks to Johnny for all the support
and special thanks to Liz for putting up with my obsession

Contents

George A. Romero:
American Maverick

'I'll never get sick of zombies. I just get sick of producers.'[1]
George Romero

It's raining in Toronto. Amidst the bad weather digital cameras roll on *Diary of the Dead*, a fifth zombie movie from legendary director George A. Romero. The budget is minuscule, the cast unknown and the location cold as hell. In the November drizzle Romero sits on his director's chair wrapped in a thick winter coat, but the wind still finds its way around his bones. He's getting old, seen too much illness, smoked too many cigarettes. Yet despite it all he is content. George Romero is where he belongs, outside the system, making films his own way. This sure beats Hollywood.

Since his debut picture *Night of the Living Dead* in 1968 he has stayed almost exclusively independent of the mainstream, allowing him to produce a fierce and uncompromised body of work. He's the director who in *Night* cast a black hero during America's worst civil rights riots – then killed him off at the bitter end. In *Day of the Dead* (1985) he attacked a Reagan-era US military and in 2000's *Bruiser* revealed the face-lessness behind his country's aspirational, 'have more' culture. For more than 25 years Romero directed his movies from Pittsburgh, an industrial American city some 2,145 miles away from Hollywood interference.

11

This is because in LA integrity is a dirty word. The studios don't get him; can't understand why he doesn't want their money. To make matters worse he directs horror pictures, a genre regarded as the mutated stepchild of decent cinema. His films are grotesque: full of ghouls grinding human flesh, slippery red gore and rancid organs. In *Dawn of the Dead* (1978) he gave cinema one of its first exploding heads and he has never backed away from the nastiness of killing. It was Romero himself who coined the term 'splatter movie'.

He is best known for his *Dead* saga, a series of films where the central antagonists are walking corpses. Zombies, as they later became known, originated as the undead slaves of Haitian voodoo and found cinematic 'life' as early as the 1930s in films like *White Zombie* (1932). But Romero single-handedly buried this interpretation and dug the creatures up as flesh-eating ghouls who bore down on their victims like a biblical plague. From 1968 onward, the living dead belonged to Romero.

Night was a seminal movie that went straight for the jugular. Fellow horror director John Carpenter holds it responsible for inspiring every single independent movie that followed. This is only a slight exaggeration and its success gave credence to other regional filmmakers like John Waters and John Sayles. In terms of horror, *Night*'s unflinching violence and enraged political agenda resurrected indie fright pictures for a modern age. Without Romero there'd be no *Last House on the Left* (1972), no *Texas Chain Saw Massacre* (1974) or *Assault on Precinct 13* (1976). Hell, there wouldn't even be *Jaws* (1975).

While the film may have turned Romero into an instant legend, it also became a millstone around his neck. From that moment his name was forever tied to horror. 'I'm trapped in a genre I love,'[2] he later admitted, and in his 40-year career only *There's Always Vanilla* (1971) and *Knightriders* (1981) properly

12

escaped the genre. But it is not just directorial typecasting that has imprisoned Romero – it is also America itself, and his own inability to look away from its dark side. Thematically his films linger in the country's shadows and then pull its monsters out for a closer look. To the US he's like some long-dead relative emerging from the grave to tell buried secrets about the family no one wants to hear.

America is Bleeding

Film critic Robin Wood described Romero as being 'rooted in the Vietnam/Watergate syndrome of disillusionment, protest and subversion'.[3] He came to prominence in the late 60s/early 70s, an era of social disintegration in the wake of John F. Kennedy's assassination. Kids were getting killed in Vietnam, there were riots on the streets and later President Nixon was caught lying and sanctioning illegal wiretaps and break-ins. Peace and love became nothing more than a nostalgic memory. The American Dream had become a nightmare and Romero knew it. In his movies the stars and stripes is more likely to be found hanging in graveyards than flying on the family porch. He politicised the horror movie.

1973's *The Crazies* deals with a biological virus accidentally unleashed on a small town. The disease sends the inhabitants mad and the army's attempts to control the situation results in slaughter. The film was made at the tail end of the Vietnam War; a period when American losses were catastrophic and the army's brutality towards Vietnamese civilians horrified the world. Romero's film shows a clear anti-military edge as faceless soldiers shoot ordinary people and bully their way into town. The film's government is separate and uncaring, happily planning to nuke the town out of existence to stop the virus spreading. Mistrust of those in control is a key theme throughout

Romero's career. Ideologically speaking, he's an anarchist and in the 1960s he wasn't alone.

The decade saw filmmakers such as Arthur Penn and Dennis Hopper get behind a new wave in American cinema, producing anti-establishment classics like *Bonnie and Clyde* (1967) and *Easy Rider* (1969). They had lost faith with government and shared Romero's fear that bloodshed was becoming their generation's defining motif. The only difference was that these directors were working with Hollywood cash – within the system – while Romero shot fast and dirty on the streets of Pittsburgh. In 1973 Romero's entire budget for *The Crazies* was $75,000 – less than Jack Nicholson's fee for starring in new-wave classic *The Last Detail* in the same year.

Romero's modern-day vampire story *Martin* (1976) was filmed for next to nothing in an industrial town during a savage American depression. It was a place left to stagnate by an impassive government and the whole town was lifeless – bled white like one of Martin's victims. This was horror vérité. In 1968, *Night of the Living Dead*'s black-and-white documentary approach added a stark realism to the narrative, which when coupled with the gut-crunching horror often proved too much for the average Saturday-night cinemagoer. Romero's films often bypass multiplexes altogether, playing best in drive-ins, midnight fleapits and on deteriorated home video. His films have an underground edge, but this is perhaps how he likes it. He is an outsider. Always has been.

George Andrew Romero was born in New York on 4th February 1940 into a multi-ethnic, devout Catholic family. Growing up a 'spic kid' in the Italian-dominated Bronx he was a loner, regularly picked on by the kids down the block. His parents sent him to Catholic school but he didn't fit in there either. His isolation turned him to the cinema – the movie theatre being the perfect place to hide alone in the dark. Romero adored the cinema and ate up anything from John Wayne westerns, Universal horror movies, sci-fi B pictures, French New Wave, Stanley Kubrick and Ingmar Bergman. He idolised Orson Welles, a director who, with films like *Citizen Kane* (1941), showed an inclination to pick at America's scabs. But Romero's most beloved was *Tales of Hoffman* (1951), Michael Powell's gaudy filmed opera in three parts. As a kid in New York, Romero rented a 16mm copy almost every week. Even then he knew he wanted to make movies.

At 14 he borrowed a rich uncle's 8mm camera and directed his first feature *The Man from the Meteor*. During the production of this 'mini epic' he experienced his first run-in with the establishment when he was arrested for throwing a burning dummy from a roof. In 1957 Romero moved to Pittsburgh to study commercial art at the Carnegie Institute of Technology, but he soon found the pull of filmmaking too strong to resist. He dropped out, acted as a gopher on Hitchcock's *North by Northwest* (1959) and later set up his own commercials business with some friends. Together they funded and produced *Night of the Living Dead*. They filmed it between beer commercials.

Hate the Living, Love the Dead

His zombies have always been a call for revolution – a new culture devouring the dysfunctional old one. In *Night* it is a racist, gun-toting society on the verge of self-destruction. In *Dawn* it's the 70s consumers obsessed by shopping and easy living. He finds horror lurking everywhere in America. It hides behind white picket fences and creeps through backyards. *Martin* brought the vampire into Middle America and 1982's *Creepshow* gave us an abusive, drunk, everyman father who slaps his kid around for reading horror comics.

Romero hits hardest at what most Americans hold dear, particularly family and religion. For him these things are at the root of all evil. At best Catholicism is ineffectual and at worst damaging. In *Martin* the title character's family are zealots (cousin Cuda keeps a 3D picture of Jesus in his kitchen) and their belief that mental illness is really a satanic possession has led to bloody atrocities. Fundamentalism has, in Martin, created a vampire. Whatever else those nuns taught Romero at Catholic school, they showed him that religion was just another authority figure not to be trusted.

Martin's family unit is central to his psychosis and Romero's films have often returned to this portrayal of troubled homes. *Monkey Shines* (1988) gives us a paraplegic whose life becomes dominated by his overbearing mother. She bathes him gently and gets jealous when he falls in love. The psychic link he has developed with a simian helper eventually leads to mom's brutal death in an electrified bathtub. To Romero, the 1950s nuclear family was nothing better than a black lie. *Season of the Witch* (1972) shows us an oppressed housewife resorting to the occult to change her way of life. Joan is unable to communicate with her teenage daughter and her husband is violent, slapping her around when their daughter runs away. Joan's family has given her nightmares and the only escape appears to be in the darkness – where the dead things are.

For the director, family, religion and government are parochial forms of control – organisations, if you will, run by stupid white men. As a result, his protagonists are often from minorities (like that 'spic kid' growing up in the Bronx). There's the black hero in *Night* and the strong female protagonists in *Day* and *Land of the Dead* (2005). These are characters displaced by society and, as a result, can better see its shortcomings. In *Knightriders* a group of bikers live an idyllic life away from the mainstream and they welcome anyone regardless of race, creed or sexuality. This nomadic community lives by a code of honour lost in the world around them.

In the 1990s Romero dipped his toe into the mainstream but found that films like *Monkey Shines* and *The Dark Half* (1992) were diluted by studio interference and quickly retreated back to the fringes. The artistic freedom he found there and the ability to explore his own thematic preoccupations make him an auteur in the Andrew Sarris sense. His films, despite the open collaboration he inspires in his crew, are uniquely his. This total control has on occasion led to self-indulgence, but, even at their worst, Romero's films contain a daring intelligence and a total willingness to experiment with the form. 2007's *Diary of the Dead* was shot entirely from a subjective, first-person point of view on digital cameras. Even at the age of 68 this old dog isn't afraid to learn a few new tricks.

As a director he is no genius, though he has created masterful works of cinema (and, with *Night*, *Martin* and *Dawn of the Dead*, the occasional masterpiece). He is too blue collar, too street level for any such grandeur. His films are unique and valuable both to cinema and society. They are parables for our time, films that work as visceral entertainments that also have something to say. A rarity in horror these days.

As an American he's on the outside (physically too, as he now claims residency and produces his films in Canada – almost as if he's fled the country's gloom like his characters at the end of *Land of the Dead*). This has given him the insight to become one of the US's most furious social commentators. And he's still at it, up there in Toronto, in the rain, chain smoking and sipping coffee. The horror genre has been a cage, yes, but he has used it to open up a vein of America's dark heart and let the blood spill out on to the screen.

Romero goes his own way – and he walks with the dead.

Analysis

In order to better understand Romero and his work we have broken our analysis of each film down into the following subsections.

Ripping Yarn: Gives a brief overview of story and character.

Making a Monster: This section looks at the making of the film and gives details that include budget, location, cast, box office, reviews of the time and production notes.

Face of Death: Examines the visual style of the movie.

The Splatter Factor: Looks at the special effects and how they were achieved.

Digging up the Dead: Offers a full analytical review of the film and explores the picture's dominant themes.

American Nightmare: Explores the socio-political context of the movie and its pertinence to US culture.

From the Vault: Contains odd/salient facts about the film.

Undead or Alive: Offers a final summation and gives a mark out of five.

Blue Collar Monsters

He began modestly. With the realisation that filmmaking was everything to him, George Romero dropped out of college and decided to set up his own commercials business. His friends John Russo, Russ Streiner and Richard Ricci were onboard too, and they called themselves The Latent Image. Money was tight, and to get started Romero tapped another five thousand dollars out of his rich uncle (the one from whom he had borrowed his first camera as a kid) and used it to buy a 16mm camera and an office overlooking Pittsburgh's Monongahela River. For a while things were tough and the group lived in borderline squalor. In winter their offices got so cold that the toilet water would freeze.

But slowly things picked up. They developed a name around Pittsburgh for producing high-quality advertisements: anything from selling Chevys to family barbeques. Romero was known as the creative one – the one who directed and edited the most successful campaigns. He had a style that conveyed information fast and hard and cut frequently to keep the action moving. His most famous commercial was *The Calgon Story*, a TV ad for detergent based on *The Fantastic Voyage* (1966): 'We've got to find out what's on those fibres!' As Image's reputation grew, so too did their ambition. Commercials were just a means to an end and they began to think about maybe making a movie. The dead were calling…

Night of the Living Dead (1968)
They Won't Stay Dead!

Crew: Director/Cinematographer/Editor: George A. Romero, Producers: Russell W. Streiner and Karl Hardman, Writers: John Russo and George A. Romero, Make-Up Effects: Hardman Associates, Inc

Cast: Duane Jones (Ben), Judith O'Dea (Barbra), Karl Hardman (Harry), Marilyn Eastman (Helen), Judith Ridley (Judy), Russell Streiner (Johnny)
96 mins

Working Titles: *Night of the Flesh Eaters, Night of the Anubis, Monster Flick*

Ripping Yarn: In a bleak American graveyard, Johnny and his sister Barbra lay a wreath on their father's grave. In the distance, between the grey headstones, a pale man is watching. As they leave, the man lunges and grabs Barbra by the throat. Johnny rushes to help but is killed in the struggle. Barbra narrowly escapes with her life and runs and hides in a nearby farmhouse. The pale man staggers after her, followed by a horde of rancid walking corpses. The dead have returned to life to eat the flesh of the living.

Into the farmhouse comes Ben, a trucker out of gas and looking for refuge. With nowhere to go he decides to turn the place into a fortress, boarding up windows and doors as best he can. Outside, the living dead surround the house and Barbra slips into a catatonic shock. From the cellar, two men, Harry and Tom, emerge. They have been hiding down there with Harry's wife Helen, his daughter Karen and Tom's girlfriend Judy. Karen has been bitten.

Harry begins to fight Ben for control and demands they barricade themselves in the cellar. A television broadcast tells of a nearby rescue station and Ben resolves to use the farm's gas pump to fill up his truck and get the group to safety. It won't be easy and the night ahead will be long. Meanwhile, over the barren farmland a posse is coming, armed and as hungry for blood as the flesh-eating ghouls they are hunting...

Making a Monster: The Latent Image crew always wanted to make a movie. Sure, making commercials was okay - it paid the bills and afforded them decent production equipment (lights, editing kit, a used 35mm camera) – but, despite this success, their hearts belonged to the cinema. One afternoon in 1967, the group descended on a local restaurant, wolfing down sandwiches, chugging beer and bitching about the commercial business. Perhaps intoxicated by booze, John Russo began to formulate an idea. What if they got ten people together and got each to kick in 600 bucks? They could make a feature film on that. The others thought it over. What had they got to lose? Romero stood up, excited like a little kid. He was gonna make a movie!

It didn't take long to assemble the ten and the Image team were joined by attorney Dave Clipper, Karl Hardman and Marilyn Eastman (co-founders of a local sound studio), investor Vince Survinski, Richard Ricci's brother Rudy and Streiner's brother Gary. Making a picture sounded like fun. Early on the group decided that horror was the perfect vehicle for their low-budget production. It was cheap, didn't need stars and had a dedicated audience desperate for scares. At the very least they'd make their money back on the drive-in circuit. Inspired, Romero turned to *Anubis,* a short story he'd written based on Richard Matheson's vampire-apocalypse novel *I Am Legend.* His tale of flesh-eating ghouls was exactly what the team (now calling themselves Image Ten) wanted and he and Russo went to work on a screenplay.

Night of the Flesh Eaters was to be a collaboration, with the entire crew watching each other's backs and picking up slack when needed. Directing initially fell to Rudy Ricci but soon switched to the more technically proficient Romero. The cast was filled with friends and members of the crew, with Hardman, Eastman and Russ Streiner all taking major parts. The central role of Ben went to African-American actor Duane Jones in an era when black performers rarely got the lead (unless, of course, your name was Sidney Poitier). According to Romero, Jones was simply the best actor they knew. Colour wasn't an issue here. Black or white, Ben was just a man, trying to do his best.

Production began in July 1967 in a farmhouse on the brink of demolition. Shooting was tough and the sporadic filming dragged them well into Pittsburgh's icy winter. In a bid to expand the undead Armageddon to a national scale, Romero and team took their cameras to Washington to film some mock news footage outside the Whitehouse. Without official permission the sequence was shot guerrilla style, with Romero keeping one eye on the scene and the other eye out for the cops.

The production – *Night of the Living Dead* as it became known – was a labour of love for all concerned. The initial $6,000 budget ballooned to around $114,000 (still minuscule for a feature), but it didn't matter. They had achieved what they set out to do – they were filmmakers.

Face of Death: Black-and-white 35mm film stock was all Image Ten could afford. But back in the 60s the news was shot on the same format and Romero used this similarity to give the film a sense of disturbing reality. On the surface, the image on screen is grainy and flat. With the lights on, the farmhouse is washed out and the surrounding countryside is harshly unromantic. He catches Pittsburgh as it really was, in real locations, and almost in a documentary style records the collapse of civilisation. It's like the crew walked in on the apocalypse and started filming. Horror had never before been this urgent.

In the darkness, however, Romero was more artistic – painting with shadows when the farmhouse lights go out. The characters get trapped within an expressionistic prison of blackness and slashes of moonlight. Hands claw their way in through the boarded windows and, when the door bursts open, Barbra's dead brother is there to pull her out into the midnight dark. Editing drew upon the avant-garde techniques of European filmmakers like Jean-Luc Godard and Ingmar Bergman, and the film uses jump cuts and reductions of time to give the narrative a jarring unease. For the first attack in the graveyard, Romero cuts over 14 times in the space of 34 seconds, ending on a gut-wrenching close up of the creature's depraved face lit by a thunderstorm. The extreme speed with which the film plunges into horror is part of its devastating impact.

The Splatter Factor: Like everything else on *Night* the special effects were done cheap by multi-tasking crew members. Marilyn Eastman was responsible for the ghouls' anaemic appearance, while Karl Hardman used mortician's wax to simulate decayed flesh. For the scene in which the dead feast on human remains, a local butcher donated slopping buckets of slaughterhouse gruel: 'I can get you entrails, I can get livers, I can get anything you want,'[1] he boasted. The grotesque close ups of the undead peeling flesh off thick bones and hungrily slurping up milky intestines shows he did not disappoint.

The film's explosions and bullet-wound effects (known as squibs) were done by production manager Vince Survinski's brother Regis and his friend Tony Pantanello. Though their working methods were questionable (they set up explosives with cigars hanging from their mouths), they got the job done. When Tom and Judy are killed in an exploding truck, Regis and Tony filled the vehicle with so much TNT and gasoline that it blew the whole thing into the air, lighting up the crisp night sky and sending fire spilling across the field.

Digging up the Dead: *Night of the Living Dead* was a vicious bite to the throat of American cinema. Free from the restraints of Hollywood, the filmmakers were able to inject a total fearlessness into their debut. The casting of a black lead, the unremitting onscreen gore and the killing of the hero at the bitter end (having survived the night, Ben is murdered by the posse, who mistake him for a ghoul: 'That's another one for the fire,' intones the sheriff) all show a film happily disregarding mainstream convention.

Despite choosing the horror genre by default, Image Ten committed themselves to creating a frenzied cinematic nightmare. From the opening shot of a desolate countryside surrounded by skeletal trees, to the burning pyre of human corpses at the conclusion, the film never lets up its nihilistic vision. It pushes us into a corner and forces us to watch as the environment closes in on our protagonists. Johnny and Barbra start on a lonely country road which turns off into a graveyard, which becomes a farm, which becomes a boarded-up house, which becomes a man alone in a locked cellar. There is no escape from the bloodshed and the death and the pungent stink of rotting bodies.

Indeed, it is a film about death and a grim futility seeps into every frame. The ghouls are us. They are friends and family members risen from the grave. Some, half-dressed or in cosy dressing gowns, have been interrupted in their daily routine while others still have burial dirt on their clothes. They are a macabre reminder of how easily death comes to us, of what we will become, of how our bodies will rot and crumble in the earth. Even their surroundings are dying as winter seizes the Pittsburgh countryside. The film gives the impression that nothing will ever grow there again.

The redneck posse treat death as a sport. They chew tobacco and take the opportunity to become local celebrities and give advice on the regional news: 'Beat 'em or burn 'em – they go up pretty easy.' Out in the fields they no longer stop and check to see who they're shooting at. Back in the farmhouse, salvation seems impossible. When Ben, Tom and Judy attempt to fill their truck with gas to get to a rescue station, an accident causes the vehicle to explode. Tom and Judy are still inside and, as the fire is reflected in Ben's wide eyes, the dead move forward and feast on the barbecued remains. Ben is alone, surrounded by dead things, watching as his only chance of escape goes up in flames.

For some critics at the time, this overpowering bleakness was too much. *Variety* referred to it as 'pornography of violence'.[2] But *Night's* boldness showed the genre could be extreme and real. The film has an anger and a hopelessness that can't be ignored and doesn't lie by suggesting everything's going to be okay. With *Night of the Living Dead* the horror movie finally grew up.

American Nightmare: In July 1967, as the cameras started rolling on *Night*, America was burning. In 100 cities throughout the country, violent race riots erupted on to the streets. Ten months later, as Romero and Russ Streiner drove a finished print to distributors in New York, civil-rights leader Martin Luther King was assassinated. Bobby Kennedy would soon follow. This was the America in which *Night of the Living Dead* was born – the most violent period in the country's history since the Civil War. It would have been untruthful if the bloodshed in *Night* had taken place off screen.

The living dead are a revolutionary new society devouring a degenerate old one. The farmhouse is a microcosm of ordinary America: a 50s nuclear family, a young couple, an independent black man and a Catholic female. Yet it is rotten to the core. The family is dysfunctional: 'We may not like living together but dying together won't solve anything.' Barbra lacks a voice and allows men, first her brother and then Ben, to control her life. For his part, Ben is intelligent and proud but has a destructive anger (surely felt by many black Americans in the 1960s) simmering inside him. He punches Barbra when she gets hysterical and shoots Cooper in cold blood. All these people feel for each other is hate and they pointlessly bicker while the world dies screaming around them. Welcome to the United States.

From the Vault: The word 'zombie' is never uttered once in Romero's debut feature. In fact, it wouldn't appear in sequels *Dawn* or *Day* either, only creeping in with part four of his *Dead* saga, *Land of the Dead*.

Undead or Alive: *Night of the Living Dead* is horror cinema as it should be: harsh, socially important, unafraid and scary as hell. The genre would never be the same again. A masterpiece. 5/5

There's Always Vanilla (1971)
They were in love… for a while it didn't matter.

Crew: Director/Cinematographer/Editor: George A. Romero, Producers: Russell W. Streiner and John A. Russo, Writer: Rudolph J. Ricci, Production Director: Vincent Survinski

Cast: Ray Laine (Chris), Judith Streiner (Lynn), Johanna Lawrence (Terri), Richard Ricci (Michael), Roger McGovern (Chris's father)
93 mins

Alternative Title: *The Affair*

Ripping Yarn: Disillusioned with his job as a session musician – 'I'm tired of hearing myself on other people's records' – hippie Chris returns to his hometown in Pittsburgh. Visiting his uptight (and married) father, Chris decides to help the old man unwind by taking him to a go-go bar and getting him laid. Later on, a drunken Chris drops in on Terri, a girl he abandoned with their infant son three years earlier.

The next day he meets Lynn, a model/actress running late for a commercial audition. To help out, Chris calls the company posing as her manager and gets her the job. Impressed with his arrogant charm Lynn spends the day with him and that night they make love in her apartment. With no money and no place to go, Chris moves in.

Lynn falls in love but Chris refuses to make a serious commitment. When she gets pregnant, his obvious devastation causes her to lie and claim she made it up. Taking on the burden alone, Lynn enters Pittsburgh's filthy downtown backstreets in search of an illegal abortion and salvation for her failing relationship...

Making a Monster: 'It was an awful experience and I care very little about it,'[3] said Romero concerning his second film as director. *There's Always Vanilla* saw the collaborative approach that had served *Night of the Living Dead* so well collapse under a barrage of creative differences and inflated egos.

Following *Night's* success Romero was terrified of getting

pigeonholed as a horror guy. After rejecting a number of ideas, including a ghoulish anthology movie, the solution presented itself in the form of local actor Ray Laine. On the verge of a move to Hollywood, Laine wanted an audition piece to show to potential agents. The result was *At Play with the Angels*, a frothy 30-minute comedy about a hippie (Laine) and his serious-minded girlfriend (played by *Night*'s Judith Streiner née Ridley). The finished short won minor regional acclaim and Romero became determined to adapt it into a feature.

Angels writer Rudy Ricci was asked to expand his screenplay to 90 minutes, but was unsure if the material would sustain the longer running time. Romero and his Latent Image cohorts held firm and, without a finished script, secured $80,000 and moved into production. Then the problems started. The film aimed to examine the 60s counter-culture revolution, but no one agreed on how to approach it. Romero wanted a romantic comedy in the vein of *The Graduate* (1967) or *Goodbye, Columbus* (1969) but others wanted a serious social drama. With no one willing to back down, the movie became increasingly confused. The group began pulling apart, debates became intense and friendships collapsed in the clash for control.

Rudy Ricci meanwhile struggled to finish the screenplay and the production ran into further trouble due to Romero's commitment to directing commercials. The film's 45-day shooting schedule expanded to over a year and an overlooked obligation to pay actors by the week dragged Latent Image towards financial ruin. Romero decided to finish by patching over unfilmed plot holes with a direct-to-camera narrative by Laine, but the damage was already done. From Romero's standpoint the film was a compromised mess. Critics agreed and the film sank without a trace at the US box office. By the time the dust settled, Romero was hungry for creative control. He would never direct a film with his Latent Image colleagues again.

Face of Death: Angered by comments that *Night of the Living Dead* looked like it was printed on army stock, Romero pulled out all the stops to make *Vanilla* look 'Hollywood'. He was only part successful. The 16mm colour film exposes the low budget, and industrial Pittsburgh lacks the glamour of LA. Yet Romero still finds beauty here. The colour is vivid and has a luxurious golden hue that feels like the film's been shot primarily at dusk. As Chris and Lynn sit in the park, eating a picnic and sharing secrets, the sunlight glistens gently through the surrounding trees. Later, as the light fades, the camera watches them walk in beautiful silhouette. It gives the film a romantic glow lacking in the narrative.

In editing, Romero would refine the disjointed rhythm utilised in *Night*. When his onscreen couple get to know one another, he cuts their answers out, reducing the sequence to just questions – 'Where are you from?', 'Are you a virgin?', 'Where did you go after that?'. Aside from giving the scene a unique pace, Romero is suggesting that the answers, for Chris at least, are unimportant. For him, courtship is a game and the conversation is irrelevant. The only important thing is the end result. He wants Lynn's body, not her mind.

Digging up the Dead: As a romantic comedy *Vanilla* fails on two counts – it is neither romantic nor comedic. A limp running gag in the first 20 minutes involving 'cutting the mustard' is the only apparent attempt at humour and by the second act the jokes have disappeared completely. This is not the fault of the cast and Laine and Streiner, both semi-professional actors, do their best to inject the film with carefree warmth. She is beautiful, sweet natured and easy to fall in love with. Laine is handsome and displays an obnoxious charm that is strangely endearing (wooing Lynn by suggesting her modelling photographs look 'a little fat').

It's just a pity his character's overt narcissism makes him so unsympathetic. Chris is a free spirit in the *Easy Rider* mould: no commitments, no home, no problem. But throughout the movie he displays a total lack of feeling for anyone but himself. When he goes to a strip club, he gets his father sex for no other reason than it'll be funny, without a thought for his doting mother back home. We find out early on that Chris abandoned his ex-girlfriend with a child. He justifies his lack of remorse by convincing himself it's not his son, but later admits to Lynn, 'There must 150 kids who look like me.'

As the film delves further into the nasty side of the hippie youth culture, Romero struggles to keep events light hearted. On the surface there's the usual array of groovy 60s chic: psychedelic tunes, go-go dancers, beads, dope and trippy dialogue ('Would you like a magical trip to a mountain somewhere?'). But underneath is a world of male dominance, infidelity and abandonment. The abortion sequence is a twisted nightmare, shot like an expressionistic horror movie and resembling the climax of *The Third Man* (1949) where Harry Lime flees through the sewers of post-war Vienna.

With abortion illegal in the United States, Lynn has no choice but to enter a backstreet surgery/tenement building. In a dirty green bedroom she is asked to strip by sweaty men with whisky breath. 'Try to relax,' her doctor tells her, clutching a dull steel instrument. 'You're gonna have a little miscarriage.' Understandably Lynn runs, and races out into a maze of unlit back alleys and pitch-black dead ends. Lynn eventually escapes the horror, but Romero was beginning to find out that, as a director, he could not.

American Nightmare: The portrayal of women in *Night* as helpless and weak willed would always trouble the usually progressive Romero. His later films all contain a strong feminist agenda and *Vanilla* displays his growing sympathy with the need for equality in the US. This demand to end sexual discrimination hit a nerve with a man who had always seen America's patriarchal society as deeply problematic.

Chris claims to be a progressive kinda guy, but he uses the sexual revolution to serve his own misogynistic purposes (as do the male advertisers Lynn works for, who appropriate the relaxed attitude to sex as another way to sell a beer). Chris is happy to live in Lynn's house and to allow her to be the sole breadwinner. When she returns from work, he also expects her to fall into the traditional role of the wife, ironing his shirts and cooking meals. Lynn's mother later expresses regret at her own marriage to a domineering husband. She tells her daughter that the secret to life isn't being 'the perfect wife', but being an independent and self-reliant woman.

From the Vault: The film was distributed by Cambist Films, a soft-porn company looking to go legit. Their other credits include *Aroused* (1966), *The Minx* (1969) and later *Ilsa, She Wolf of the SS* (1975).

Undead or Alive: Whereas *Vanilla* template *The Graduate* was able to comment on sexual liberation without losing its sense of humour, Romero's film sinks into the era's rotten underbelly with barely a smile. As his films go, it is not his strongest. 1/5

Season of the Witch (1972)
Every night is Halloween.

Crew: Director/Writer/Cinematographer/Editor: George A. Romero, Producers: Nancy M. Romero & Gary Streiner, Production Supervisor: Vincent Survinski, Music: Steve Gorn, Song: 'Season of the Witch' by Donovan

Cast: Jan White (Joan), Ray Laine (Gregg), Anne Muffly (Shirley), Joedda McClain (Nikki), Bill Thunhurst (Jack), Virginia Greenwald (Marion)
104 mins

Alternative Titles: *Jack's Wife, Hungry Wives*

Ripping Yarn: Joan is a middle-class housewife for whom the clock is ticking. Her husband Jack is domineering and she can no longer communicate with her grown-up daughter Nikki. She feels like a prisoner caged behind a white picket fence. At a party, Joan's bridge partner Shirley tells her of a woman who performs tarot readings in town. She says she's a witch.

Joan accompanies Shirley to a reading and becomes fascinated with witchcraft. Later that night, they return to Joan's house to find Nikki with her on/off boyfriend Gregg. He expresses a cynicism towards the occult, arguing that suggestion is much more powerful. He demonstrates his point by convincing Shirley that an ordinary cigarette is grass, and they watch as she gets high. Joan drives Shirley home and returns to hear Nikki and Gregg making love. On finding her mother back, Nikki is appalled and leaves home.

When Joan's husband goes away on business she begins to experiment with the occult. She buys ceremonial instruments and casts spells to draw Gregg to her. They have sex surrounded by burning black candles. Joan's dabbling becomes more serious and her dreams are haunted by a prowler in black with the face of the god Pan. Reality and nightmare become hard to tell apart. She is alone in her perfect suburban home, and the darkness is closing in…

Making a Monster: The break-up between Romero's *Night of the Living Dead* and *There's Always Vanilla* collaborators had been messy and the former friends were now communicating through lawyers. But unchained from the shackles of committee filmmaking, Romero was at last free to make whatever film he wanted. That film would be *Jack's Wife*, a feminist diatribe about an oppressed housewife. Worried that potential investors would be put off by the film's art-house aspirations, Romero filled the screenplay with titillating scenes of sex and horror that he never intended to shoot. A deal was eventually struck with a brokerage firm that guaranteed $750,000 for his next three pictures.

Jack was budgeted at $250,000 and Romero secured a $100,000 bank loan to get things started. Once again he would shoot in his beloved Pittsburgh and rounded up a crew of friends that included his then wife Nancy. In casting, he utilised contacts from the advertising world and here found soap opera and commercials actress Jan White for the lead. *There's Always Vanilla's* heartthrob Ray Laine took the part of Gregg, the object of Joan's lustful fixation. With everything in place and cameras rolling, Romero was hit with a bombshell – his brokerage investors had gone bankrupt.

The director would have to make a $250,000 movie for only one hundred thousand. On top of that he now had a hefty bank loan and no way of paying it back. He refused to give up. Making movies was his life, and neither money nor debt could stop him. He ploughed forward, but *Jack's Wife* would suffer as a result. Scenes were shortened or removed, production values sacrificed and scope narrowed.

On completion the film was picked up by distributor Jack Harris who decided that a talky art picture was unsellable. Reducing the running time from 130 to 89 minutes, Harris renamed the movie *Hungry Wives* and tried to sell it as a soft-porn flick. The trailer emphasised the movie's brief sex scenes with a flirtatious female voice announcing, '*Hungry Wives*... with an appetite for diversion.' Romero was appalled, but it was basically the same trick he had used when selling the screenplay. As a porn movie with no real sex and a feminist edge, *Hungry Wives* magically disappeared at the box office.

Following the success of *Dawn of the Dead* in 1978, *Jack's Wife* was re-released and retitled to capitalise on Romero's acclaim. Now called *Season of the Witch* and marketed solely at the horror crowd, the film still struggled to find an audience. It was Romero's second movie in a row that nobody wanted to see.

Face of Death: Although *Night* benefited from Romero's low-down approach to cinematography, *Witch*'s bleached visuals and dirty 16mm blow up undermined the narrative's suburban prosperity. It is perhaps his most ugly film. The colours are washed out and the gaudy 70s décor adds an unpleasant busy-ness to the frame. Romero shot the film himself and displayed an inexperience towards the rules of moviemaking (after all, he never had any formal training and was, as always, basically making it up as he went along). The camera constantly breaks the 180-degree rule, confusing the film's geography and ensuring characters' eye-lines don't meet.

However, Romero had a natural talent and the film does boast some remarkable set pieces. When Joan purchases occult knives and chalices, the sequence becomes a beautifully shot montage playing out to Donovan's 'Season of the Witch'. The scene builds to a crescendo and ends with Joan's first experiments with witchcraft. It is a neat centre point to the film and gives way to the darker second half of magick and murder. Then there is Joan's nightmare of a rapist god breaking into her home. He crashes through locked doors and plunges into the foreground, filling the moonlit frame with his grinning mask. The scene is another of Romero's black kaleidoscopes of terror.

Digging up the Dead: Of all his films, Romero claims that *Witch* is the one he'd most like to remake. It is easy to see why. Despite the grubby visuals, dated production values (dig the flowery green wallpaper and dresses, man) and weak supporting performances the film offers a pertinent study of everyday oppression and prosperous middle-class suburbia. Joan has a beautiful house, expensive clothes and lavish jewellery. She attends smug dinner parties and plays bridge with her self-satisfied friends. Yet she is totally alienated from everyone around her. She watches herself grow older in the giant bedroom mirror and listens, almost hypnotised, to the ticking of the downstairs clock. Her husband is uninterested in a meaningful physical relationship and she is jealous of her daughter's youth. In one of the film's more disturbing sequences, she becomes sexually aroused at the sound of Nikki making love and longs to be with her daughter's sexual partner.

Romero approaches the film's supernatural elements sceptically and we are never sure if the magic is real. Joan casts spells to draw Gregg to her, but also calls him and invites him over just to make sure; 'I find that my evening is free,' she tells him. Was it magic or Gregg's own sexual openness that brought him to her? Romero keeps things ambiguous, allowing the film to work as a character study instead of an outright horror.

Joan's belief in black sorcery could point to the tangible existence of evil, or it could be the product of a distressed mind searching for meaning. Jan White is excellent in the lead role and her glassy detachment as she crawls deeper into the realms of the occult further hints at a possible mental breakdown.

Sadly, the reliance on dialogue and lengthy philosophical debate makes for an intermittently dull movie-going experience. A late-night drink with Gregg, Nikki and Shirley throws into question the reality of witchcraft, the mind's capacity to believe, life, the universe and everything in it. These scenes are wordy and bear all the insight of a doped-up student discussion. More interesting, given that this was Romero's first solo film away from Latent Image, is just how in sync it is with his previous efforts. The social consciousness, the dynamic camera and the editing all mirror *Night* and *Vanilla*. The three films sit nicely together, the work of a manic and fearless regional auteur.

American Nightmare: Picking up from the feminist stirrings of *There's Always Vanilla*, Romero's third film would become a full-blown discourse on gender revolution. The early 70s was a traumatic time for minorities and the feminist movement became vocal about an end to sexual discrimination. In *Witch*, Jack is the dominant breadwinner and master of his domain. In an avant-garde dream sequence, we see him leading his wife around on a leash, and later, when Joan fails to discipline Nikki, he hits her – like he's training a dog. Witchcraft appears to be her only way out.

But the magic becomes another prison. Joan's problem is that she refuses to take responsibility for her actions and she is looking for an excuse to murder her way to freedom. 'The Devil made me do it' is apparently what she is saying. The film ends with her initiation into a witch's coven where she is stripped naked and a silk leash is put around her neck by the High Priestess. Refusing to take control of her existence, one form of oppression has replaced another.

From the Vault: Cast and crew claimed the shoot was besieged by weird phenomena. When Joan writes the Lord's Prayer backwards, the film stock repeatedly came back warped. At the film's conclusion, as Joan announces 'I'm a witch,' a huge crack opened up above her head and split the ceiling in two. Audiences may have ignored *Season of the Witch* but, according to the crew, the Devil did not.

Undead or Alive: A movie 'torn between genre and art'[4], as one critic put it. *Season of the Witch* is fun, pretentious, ugly, exciting, dull, scary and, above all, worthwhile. A grungy alternative to *Rosemary's Baby* (1968) and *The Exorcist* (1973). 3/5

The Crazies (1973)
Why are the good people dying?

Crew: Director/Editor: George A. Romero, Producer: A.C. Croft, Production Screenplay: George A. Romero, based on the screenplay by Paul McCollough, Cinematographer: S. William Hinzman, Music: Bruce Roberts, Song: 'Heaven Help Us' by Beverly Bremers

Cast: Lane Carroll (Judy), W.G. McMillan (David), Harold Wayne Jones (Clank), Lloyd Hollar (Col Peckem), Lynn Lowry (Kathy), Richard Liberty (Artie), Richard France (Dr Watts) 98 mins

Alternative Titles: *Mad People, Code Name: Trixie*

Ripping Yarn: In an isolated American farmhouse, a young boy frightens his sister by pretending to be a zombie. Upstairs, their father has gone berserk. He kills their mother and sets fire to the house. David, a volunteer fireman, heads to the scene, while his nurse girlfriend, Judy, is called to surgery. On arrival she finds the place overrun by armed soldiers in gasmasks and white decontamination suits. The local doctor tells her that a plane transporting a contagious virus has crashed nearby. Those infected either die or go totally mad.

The military places the town under quarantine. Judy is pregnant and the doctor tells her to find David and leave Evans City. Soldiers begin rounding up civilians, breaking into homes and dragging people on to the streets. Some townsfolk are armed and a bloody war develops. David and his old army buddy Clank find Judy but are soon captured along with local man Artie and his daughter Kathy.

The virus co-creator Dr Watts arrives and reveals that the disease is a military weapon for which there is no cure and, as the plague spreads, the government considers nuking the town out of existence. David, Judy and the others escape and decide to head past the quarantine line. Evans City has become a living hell. Murder and disease is rampant, the town is under martial law and it has become impossible to tell who is sane and who is crazy...

Making a Monster: *The Crazies* should have been Romero's easiest production. Unlike his previous movies, which he'd had to beg, borrow and steal to get made, this film already had a budget and distributor. It even had a first draft of the screenplay. Entitled *Mad People* and written by Paul McCollough, the apocalyptic story drew interest from Lee Hessel who agreed to finance the film but with some changes. He wanted an action-packed thriller, but McCollough wanted something more allegorical. As their relationship broke down, the writer sold the idea to producer A.C. Croft who brought Romero onboard to rewrite. He removed everything but the first three pages.

Narrowing the scope to a singular American town, Romero was able to draw maximum potential out of the claustrophobic narrative and meagre $225,000 budget. Shooting took place in Evans City, a backwater town in Nowheresville, Pennsylvania. Here things got difficult. When a scene called for the partial nudity of actor Lloyd Hollar, the redneck faction of the town threatened to bring production to a stop. The brief display of skin didn't bother them – it was the fact the skin was black that they objected to. Romero's status as a local somehow managed to appease them.

The rest of the cast was filled out by a number of offbeat performers, particularly elfin cult actress Lynn Lowry (star of David Cronenberg's *Shivers* [1974]) and the formidable Richard France as Dr Watts. France is a bear of a man, but urbane and scholarly with it. His hair and beard are a pristine black, his belly wide and his voice bass in the Orson Welles key. He delivers lines of apocalyptic warning – 'It's in the water, man! Underground!' – with a thunderous onscreen presence.

Behind the camera, Romero, for the first time, employed someone else as cinematographer, and friend William 'Bill' Hinzman was hired to lens the picture. Shot over a tight 40 days during a bitter winter, the crew shot guerrilla fashion, doing 40 camera set-ups through 12-18 hour days – 'Grab the shots, man. Light 'em as quick as you can,'[5] yelled Romero like a man possessed. The breakneck production eventually took a toll on his health and a diseased gall bladder put him in hospital not long after the movie was completed.

On the plus side, Lee Hessel flipped for *The Crazies* – loved it. Money was poured into a big release and a huge cut-out soldier stood proudly in Times Square, New York. No one showed. Romero's third flop in a row. His health shot, deep in debt and without a successful movie since *Night*, the director was spent. He wouldn't make another movie for three years.

Face of Death: A military drum pounds over the soundtrack, the images cut sharply to its rapid pace. A door is cracked open. Soldiers barge in on a family home. A mother and baby are forced out of bed. A woman willing to cooperate has a rifle stuck in her face. Soldiers steal household possessions. A man goes for his guns. The military drum continues to pound. With *The Crazies*, Romero's jagged editing technique went full tilt and the film hits like a machinegun barrage of static frames. The effect is frantic and, coupled with the staccato soundtrack, drills the army's brutal omnipresence into the landscape.

Romero's use of framing and brash colour drew upon EC Comics like *Tales from the Crypt* and *Vault of Horror*, comics he had secretly adored as a kid. These lurid horror tales would be a source of inspiration throughout his career. The colours in *The Crazies* are bold, aggressive and gaudy. In one standout sequence a smiling grandmother repeatedly sinks her knitting needle deep into a soldier's chest, watching as he becomes entangled in the green yarn. The contrast between the soldier's white tunic and the slaughterhouse red that flows out of his body is startling. The old lady, meanwhile, goes on with her knitting.

Digging up the Dead: After five years of trying to escape, *The Crazies* was another unwitting step back into horror. Romero called the movie a science-fiction thriller in the vein of *Invasion of the Body Snatchers* (1955) or *The Andromeda Strain* (1971) but the film is too unflinching to properly fit that label.

Yes, it shares *Andromeda's* caustic look at biological weapons and *Body Snatchers'* small-town paranoia, but there is also real darkness here. As David and his friends escape across the countryside they encounter all manner of insanities. A woman sweeps up blood in a field with a broom; Artie has sex with his daughter and then hangs himself; and dead bodies are dumped in trash bags and burned.

The army are an invading force and treat resisting civilians as enemies. They never explain what they are doing and appear almost inhuman behind black, dead-eyed gasmasks. It is only a matter of time before things get ugly. 'You ain't taking me no place!' cries a disturbed farmer as he uses a shotgun to paint sloppy red on to a white human canvas. He is either crazy or frightened – the soldiers don't know and don't care and he is executed along with the rest of them. The politicians in charge are unconcerned by the gross loss of human life and there is a sort of *Dr Strangelove* (1963) style madness as they make decisions over a working lunch. 'If we have to push the button,' says one about dropping a nuclear weapon on the city, 'we'll just say the bomb went off.'

In many ways the film is a reworking of *Night of the Living Dead*, with faceless soldiers replacing walking corpses. Themes of mistrust and social collapse mirror Romero's debut and the film even knowingly begins in the same manner, with a brother scaring his sister and then being exposed to a genuine threat – in this case their infected father. Replacing *Night's* monster with a human menace makes the film more direct in its attack on a corrupt America.

Also, like *Night*, *The Crazies* is angry, and the political callousness and military bureaucracy both lead towards a cynical and unresolved conclusion. The virus spreads to another town, a scientist with a potential cure is accidentally killed and David, whose immunity to the disease could present another antidote, is ignored by those in charge. At the film's conclusion he is shoved into the high-school gym and surrounded by a mass of people steadily going out of their minds. If this isn't horror, then nothing is.

American Nightmare: The war in Vietnam was still raging, but America was beginning to realise this was a battle they could not win. The country's youth were being obliterated. 'Every day the *Six O'clock News* showed the pain of mutilation and war in our living rooms,'[6] stated Romero. America had become traumatised. These images also included atrocities committed by US troops. 'You never know what you're doing or why you do it,' observes one soldier in *The Crazies*. 'You just do it.' These could have been the words of any soldier in Vietnam ordered to torch a local village and leave kids homeless or worse.

The war's horror seeped into every aspect of the film's pungent mise-en-scène. The self-immolation of a Buddhist monk in Saigon and a peaceful anti-war protest met with gunfire at Kent State find literal expression here. David, the film's nominal hero, is an ex-Green Beret who worries about the army's ability to 'turn a campus protest into a shooting war.' Earlier, when the troops turn over a church, the Catholic priest reacts by dousing himself in kerosene and setting light to his body. As his skin peels and blackens, Romero's camera is unflinching, capturing the scene with documentary-style detachment – just like the news. The America of *The Crazies* is one of bloodshed and death. And it all plays out to the sound of 'When Johnny Comes Marching Home'.

From the Vault: Cinematographer Bill Hinzman was already a part of Romero legend after appearing as that iconic first Karloff-like ghoul at the start of *Night of the Living Dead*. He also played the masked dream god in *Season of the Witch* and a mad gunman in *The Crazies*.

Undead or Alive: A savage and brilliant indictment of a broken America. Today, in an age of government lies, pointless war and biological terrorism, *The Crazies* is as pertinent as ever. Chilling. 4/5

Weird Fantasies and Tales of Fear

Romero was in debt to the tune of about half a million dollars. His films post-*Night* had all sunk at the box office and continuing to make movies independently from Pittsburgh was beginning to seem impossible. But there was hope on the horizon. During a promotional campaign for *The Crazies* Romero met a young journalist with a degree in business. His name was Richard Rubinstein and he wanted to produce movies. Together the two men created Laurel Entertainment, a minor production company, with the intention of funding Romero's projects. First though, there was the matter of his debt. Romero refused to declare bankruptcy because he didn't want to let down the people he owed, so Rubinstein hit upon the idea of making sports profiles to boost their funds.

Over the next three years, Laurel produced around seventeen one-hour TV episodes called *The Winners*, a programme that showcased everyone from Reggie Jackson to LA Lakers basketball star Kareem Abdul-Jabbar. The most popular, *Juice on the Loose* (1974), focused on the athletic achievements of American footballer O.J. Simpson (long before his days of black gloves and low-speed police chases). Here Romero was able to hone his skills as a director and further develop his visceral style. The documentaries also took him out of Pittsburgh and he travelled America with Rubinstein and a small crew.

It would take until 1980 for Romero to fully pay off his debts but, in the meantime, he and Rubinstein had raised enough cash to consider a return to movies. Romero took his camera back into Pittsburgh, and within the urban ghettos he went looking for a vampire.

Martin (1976)
He could be the boy next door.

Crew: Director/Writer/Editor: George A. Romero, Producer: Richard Rubinstein, Cinematographer: Michael Gornick, Composer: Donald Rubinstein, Special Effects: Tom Savini

Cast: John Amplas (Martin), Lincoln Maazel (Cuda), Christine Forrest (Christina), Elyane Nadeau (Mrs Santini), Tom Savini (Arthur)
91 mins

Treatment Title: *Blood*

Ripping Yarn: A downcast teenager boards a train to Pittsburgh. Inside he sees a beautiful woman travelling alone and that night breaks into her cabin, drugs her, rapes her and drinks her blood. He is an 84-year-old vampire. His name is Martin.

At the station he is met by his elderly cousin Cuda and together they travel to his home in Braddock. Martin is the family shame – Nosferatu – an evil burden that must be carried by the devout family. 'First I will save your soul,' Cuda tells Martin. 'Then I will destroy you.' Cuda's granddaughter Christina isn't so sure. To her, Martin is simply a mixed-up kid disturbed by family superstition. Garlic doesn't work, crosses have no effect and he casts a reflection in mirrors. To earn his keep he delivers groceries around town and on his route meets

Mrs Santini, a bored housewife who hires him to do odd jobs. They begin an affair.

Martin's thirst for blood is uncontrollable but he is careful about not getting caught. He watches people, knows what they do. In a wealthy neighbourhood he attacks a woman and her lover, but without incisors to penetrate the flesh he uses needles and a razor blade. Cuda arranges for an exorcism and an aged priest tries to purify Martin's soul. But this broken city is the kind of place where monsters thrive. Cuda gives his cousin one warning: take no one from the town. It's a rule that's about to be broken…

Making a Monster: Following his three-year hiatus, Romero was hungry to return to movies. A sequel to *Night of the Living Dead* was already in the works, but as Laurel's first feature Romero needed something more affordable. The result was *Martin*. Intended as a comedy about a Dracula figure living in the modern world, the more research he did on vampirism, the more horrific his treatment became. Stories of the LA Slasher, a serial killer who drank his victims' blood, and a fourteenth-century family of Scottish thieves who lived on human flesh infused Martin with a twisted psychology that left little room for laughs.

With a budget of around $100,000, the crew consisted of only 15 close friends. These included producer Richard Rubinstein, sound designers Michael Gornick and Tony Buba (himself a skilled documentarian) and actress Christine Forrest. The divorced Romero had known Forrest since *Season of the Witch* and, while hanging out together in New York, they fell in love. He wrote a part just for her. With the *Martin* crew so close, a relaxed atmosphere developed as they leisurely shot on the streets of Braddock, Pennsylvania from summer to winter. The nightmare productions of *There's Always Vanilla* and *The Crazies* seemed a long way away.

For the title role Romero cast 27-year-old actor John Amplas, a gangly looking kid he had seen in the play *Philemon* at the Pittsburgh Playhouse. Once again, Romero was cinematographer, but the attention to set-ups was diverting him from the performances in what was essentially a character piece. Romero turned to Gornick and asked him if he wanted to shoot. He said yes and stayed on as Romero's cinematographer for the next nine years.

The first cut ran two and three quarter hours. Finding it painful to reduce the running time, Romero began a crusade for longer movies that eventually resulted in the overblown *Knightriders* in 1981. This said, the reduced version of *Martin* drew critical acclaim, with *Newsweek* calling it 'the most original horror movie in years'.[1] In 1978 *Martin* played at an independent film festival (which later became known as Sundance) and won second prize in the Drama category (losing out to Claudia Weill's little-seen *Girlfriends*). Despite its critical success the film struggled to find a mass audience. It did, however, put Romero's career firmly back on track, and with *Martin* finished he could begin to focus on his next project – *Dawn of the Dead*.

Face of Death: Romero considered releasing *Martin* in black and white but distribution pressures ensured the colour version remained. It is to the film's benefit. The grainy 16mm blow up is more street level, with the bloodless palette of dirty greys and browns emphasising the squalor of a dying city. Indoors, things are equally vacant. The interior of Cuda's house is whitewashed and he himself wears a pure white suit that alludes to his self-appointed grandeur as God's avenging angel. Only in death does the film shimmer with full colour as the rich blood from Martin's victims spills out free and easy. 'The blood is the life,' as Béla Lugosi's Dracula once said.

Martin is punctuated by otherworldly flashbacks to a Gothic Victorian age, where he pursues willing victims and flees from villagers bearing flaming torches. Romero grew up watching reruns of classic Universal monster movies on TV, where Lugosi's Count prowled dripping Transylvanian catacombs. Martin's flashbacks stemmed from these. In some ways it's also like an inverted *Wizard of Oz* (1939), where the colour reality is dismal and the black and white glows with a dreamlike elegance. This contrast is best displayed in the standout opening sequence. Martin breaks into the compartment of a beautiful female passenger and imagines what waits for him inside. His vision is sumptuous as his victim greets him in a flowing white gown and with open arms. But the colour reality is a flushing toilet, a face pack and a snotty nose. Martin's attack is unforgiving and far from romantic.

The Splatter Factor: A young kid wanders into Romero's office to audition for the part of Martin. He has brought a portfolio of photographs showing him made up as various monsters. He did the effects himself. The title role has already been cast but Romero likes what he sees and Tom Savini is welcomed into the family. He quickly gets to work slicing wrists and shooting heads, bringing an unchained enthusiasm to his work as a one-man cinematic slaughterhouse (albeit one who uses latex and foam rubber rather than a butcher's knife). He's like a showman at a macabre carnival: 'It's a study for me. It's my art, my life. This is what I do.'[2]

The reality he brought to these special effects disturbed many. The crew filmed in the house of Tony Buba's grandmother and, during the climactic scene where Martin is staked through the heart, the old lady thought John Amplas had actually been murdered. Savini could only smile with glee. When an effect called for a man's throat to be pierced with a sharpened stick,

Romero considered plunging a piece of wood into a lamb's neck. But Savini talked him out of it and produced a convincing false body and neck to be placed under the actor's head. The effect came off and a beautiful working relationship developed. The kid even got to act in the movie and Romero cast him as Christina's boyfriend Arthur.

Digging up the Dead: 'There is no magic. It's just a sickness.' Like *Night of the Living Dead*, George Romero's *Martin* would dig up a decrepit monster and resurrect it for the modern age. In 1974 Hammer Studios released *The Legend of the Seven Golden Vampires,* a campy last entry into their *Dracula* saga. The vampire was losing its hypnotic power and becoming just another dusty antique in its ruinous castle. Romero took a different approach – he moved the monster in next door. Martin's the quiet kid down the street: awkward and lonely behind lank hair and watching, cat-like eyes. He wanders through the crumbling streets with his head down and hands in his pockets. He is one of us.

This sense of mundane reality made *Martin* one of the most shocking and disturbing horror movies of the 1970s. Romero strips the vampire of his mystical powers and leaves nothing but an insatiable thirst. Unlike Dracula there is no eroticism to his attacks, only frightened women struggling for their lives. His first victim calls him a 'freak rapist asshole', which indeed he is, but one who needs blood to survive. His method is plausible and matter-of-fact. He knocks her out with an injection, undresses her and slices her vein with a razor. The flow of blood over his naked body fills him with orgasmic ecstasy and he cleans up afterwards with clinical precision.

Catholicism has no power over Martin. Crucifixes don't work and an exorcism is ineffective. Braddock's church has long since burnt down and Sunday mass takes place in a filthy warehouse. The city has been abandoned and the Church holds little meaning to its faithful, let alone its demons. The lack of traditional magic on display brings into question whether Martin is a supernatural entity at all. Christina thinks he's delusional: 'He's unbalanced – he's mad and you... have driven him to it,' she tells the Van Helsing-like Cuda. He claims that family records show proof but Romero, like with *Season of the Witch*, refuses to let go of the narrative's ambiguity. The result is a film that can be viewed as either a straight vampire tale or the story of a screwed-up kid damaged by his own family.

In both cases Martin is oddly sympathetic, remarkable considering his murderous actions, and John Amplas delivers a downtrodden performance of subtle beauty. With Mrs Santini, he is wide-eyed and curious and he reminds her of an alley cat she once had: 'He used to sit on the floor and stare up at me with those eyes,' she tells him. He's gentle and softly spoken. But as he stalks his victims his eyes become focused and he transforms from shy kid to detached killer in the blink of an eye. As Romero himself says, 'Martin is truly a dangerous creature; he has us all figured out, while we haven't come close to understanding him.'[3] He is a 'vampire for our age of disbelief' and his frank plausibility makes for many a sleepless suburban night.

American Nightmare: America was in the midst of its most devastating economic crisis since the Great Depression and the once thriving steel town of Braddock had been hit hard. The mills were closed, factories boarded up and workers tossed on to the streets to fend for themselves. It became a town of stray dogs and broken promises. 'There was this sadness about it,' Romero observed. 'People were still sitting in the taverns waiting for [the mills] to reopen. The American dream was crumbling.'[4]

His camera follows Martin through a town left to rot by a floundering US government. He wanders past smashed shops and puke-soaked alleys. As the film draws to a close and his thirst deepens, he stalks the homeless, needle-stuck junkies in search of a victim no one will miss. Braddock is full of them. Those able to do so have left town long ago. Eventually he stumbles across two destitute drunks looking for a place to sleep and cuts them open with a broken bottle. Braddock had become another of Romero's graveyards.

From the Vault: Almost all of Romero's films contain blink-and-you'll-miss-it cameos from the director. With *Martin*, short on funds, Romero cast himself as the boozy young priest Father Howard: 'I don't suppose it's sacrilege to say the wine at St Vincent's is putrid.' He does a pretty good job.

Undead or Alive: *Martin* showed a growing professionalism in Romero's work and a deeper understanding of the film-making process. His modernisation of the vampire mythology is stark, hard-hitting and relevant. It is Romero's favourite of his own films. 5/5

Dawn of the Dead (1978)
When there's no more room in
Hell the dead will walk the earth.

Crew: Director/Writer/Editor: George A. Romero, Producer: Richard P. Rubinstein, Cinematographer: Michael Gornick, Sound: Tony Buba, Music: The Goblins with Dario Argento, Special Make-Up Effects: Tom Savini

Cast: David Emge (Stephen), Ken Foree (Peter), Scott H. Reiniger (Roger), Gaylen Ross (Francine), David Crawford

(Dr Foster), David Early (Mr Berman), Richard France (Scientist)
127 mins

Alternative Titles: *Dawn of the Living Dead* (working title), *Zombies* (Europe)

Ripping Yarn: America is in a state of emergency. The dead still walk and their numbers grow larger by the day. In the midst of the chaos a Pennsylvanian TV station continues to broadcast, directing people to rescue stations long since closed down. Seeing their situation as hopeless, weather reporter Stephen steals a helicopter and persuades his PA girlfriend Fran to go with him. They plan to head north to Canada and are later joined by SWAT operatives Roger and Peter.

The group travel throughout the night, passing farmlands where rednecks happily mow down the undead. With fuel and supplies running low they descend on a shopping complex and decide to get what they need from inside. Zombies overrun the place. Stephen needs rest and they decide to hole up in the mall's loft space, but for Peter the opportunity below is too great to pass up. 'Let's go shopping,' he suggests. They head down into the mall and stock up on essentials. The place has everything they need and Peter sees its potential as a place to stay.

Using nearby trucks they block off the mall entrances. Roger is bitten but the group continue to fight for their new home and they wipe out all the zombies inside. The place is theirs and Fran reveals that she is pregnant. Days and weeks merge. In the distance an army of scavenger bikers see the mall and decide that they too want what's inside…

Making a Monster: Monroeville Mall, Pittsburgh, 1974. Owner Mark Mason is showing his buddy George around one of the first shopping complexes in America. It's his pride and joy, complete with stores of every description. The tour concludes with a look at the crawl spaces above the ceiling. 'People could probably survive up there,'[5] suggests Mark. His buddy George Romero thinks for a second. Survive what?

Romero had resisted a sequel to *Night of the Living Dead* for over five years but the idea of a mall overrun by zombies took over his imagination. He began to formulate an action-orientated script and early on decided that this would be part two of a trilogy that sees the dead take over the world. Italian horror maestro Dario Argento (director of *Deep Red* [1975] and *Suspiria* [1976]) agreed to co-finance the $640,000 budget in return for foreign rights and a European cut, and Romero finished the screenplay in Rome with Argento consulting. The final draft came to over 253 pages.

The *Dawn* crew was an extension of the team behind *Martin* and the family atmosphere was pivotal in completing what was essentially a Hollywood blockbuster filmed on a micro-budget. Casting took place in New York and here they found all the film's principal stars. Scott Reiniger and David Emge tossed burgers together in the same restaurant; Ken Foree knew *Night* actor Duane Jones; and Gaylen Ross faked her acting résumé to get the job. Mason allowed Romero to shoot in his beloved mall and in late 1977 they began shooting at night between opening hours. Despite their lack of sleep the enthusiastic crew brought a vital energy to the production and managed to get by on nothing more than coffee and cookies. As shooting progressed, Romero's improvisational style saw a more comedic tone creep in. Gags were added and the downbeat ending where Fran and Peter commit suicide was replaced with their more optimistic escape. *Dawn of the Dead* took on a life all of its own.

A 139-minute version premiered at the Cannes Film Festival

in 1978, but for the European release Argento reduced the movie to 118 minutes, cutting much of the humour he felt would be lost on foreign audiences. He also had his *Suspiria* collaborators The Goblins provide a funk-induced heat-beat score, which Romero later applied to his own version. Back in the US, censors the MPAA deemed the film's ultra-violent content worthy of an X, a rating usually reserved for hardcore porn. This meant a limited audience and prohibited advertising. Romero's refusal to distil his vision saw major distributors steer clear and *Dawn* wouldn't appear in America for nearly a year.

Eventually Salah Hassanein's United Film Distribution Company (UFD) backed the film and released it unrated in April 1979. *Dawn* was an instant hit. Roger Ebert called it the 'ultimate horror film'[6] and it grossed $55 million world-wide. Romero's faith in his project paid off and he was lauded as an uncompromising filmmaker who could single-handedly rival Hollywood. He had gained a new power and respect – he could do anything. His next film *Knightriders* would throw all of that away for good.

Face of Death: Abandoning the black-and-white vérité of its predecessor, *Dawn of the Dead* is a full-on visual attack in unliving colour. Like *The Crazies*, the film is one big EC comic, full of macabre humour and lashings of Grand Guignol (in the mall a sombrero-wearing biker takes a blood test before the zombies show up and give his blood a test of their own). Each shot is a moving panel of off-kilter angles and weird close ups, all painted in block primary colours. The undead are pale blue with blood like melted red crayon and SWAT operatives Roger and Peter dress in majestic navy uniforms that make them look like superheroes as they slide down ropes and punch out zombies.

In some ways this mix of action and extravagant texture

makes it feel like the 1938 Technicolor classic *The Adventures of Robin Hood,* with Ken Foree as a sort of ghetto Errol Flynn. It is to Romero's credit that, despite bringing the horror out into the mall's Day-Glo lights, the film never loses its sense of terror. The zombies pose a very real threat and the sheer visceral power of their attacks keeps the film firmly in the realms of nightmare. The sight of a zombie biting a thick chunk of flesh off a loved one's neck or a thumb being pushed deep into a bite wound makes the film as much an endurance test for the stomach as anything else.

The Splatter Factor: 'Hey, we've got another gig – start thinking of ways to kill people,'[7] read Romero's telegram to Tom Savini. Savini took it to heart and, with *Dawn,* cemented his reputation as one of the most inventive special-effects wizards of the modern age. The film contains innumerable scenes of appalling magic: the top of a zombie's head is sliced off by a helicopter rotor blade, a man's intestines are clawed out, heads are chopped off and bodies are torn apart. Savini had been a combat photographer in Vietnam, capturing death through the detached lens of his camera. It was an experience that deeply unsettled him. 'Much of my work for *Dawn of the Dead* was like a series of portraits of what I'd seen for real,' he told an interviewer. 'Perhaps that's one way of working out that experience.'[8]

Savini was a vital part of *Dawn's* success and his ability to create effects cheaply in the space of hours perfectly matched Romero's gonzo ethos. When a scene was needed to fill in a continuity error, Savini immediately devised a covering 'gag', which involved Roger removing a screwdriver from a Worker Zombie's tool belt and plunging it into his ear. To Savini the mall was a huge playground where every night was like Halloween.

Digging up the Dead: A SWAT team storms a tenement building in a Hispanic project, rounding up civilians who refuse to release their dead to the authorities. Wooley, an over-weight member of Roger's command, is psyched. He boots open a door and unthinkingly shoots a homeowner in the face, exploding his head into a thousand wet pieces. Audiences in 1979 were waiting for the camera to cut away, but Romero never does. He captures everything. And this was all in the first ten minutes.

Dawn of the Dead is one of the most audacious genre movies to emerge out of American cinema. Horror had never before been so unrelentingly bloody, so adventurous and so colourful. Romero's decision to eschew darkness for a comic-book humour emphasised the film's principle agenda as a hell-bent satire. *Dawn* openly targets the consumer craze that engulfed late-1970s America, where millions of people became stricken with the need to own more stuff. 'Why do they come here?' asks Fran on seeing the mall's undead residents. 'Some kind of instinct, memory of what they used to be,' replies Stephen. 'This was an important place in their lives.' The zombies are the natural extension of everyday greed; they've simply swapped buying commodities for biting flesh.

Following *Night*, the living dead are now in a further state of putrescence (a bald, plaid-shirt-wearing zombie has a blood-clotted face with an eye bulging out of its socket) but as they pratfall off balconies and take custard pies with (literally) dead-pan perfection, they come to resemble an army of rotting Buster Keatons – albeit ones more likely to slip on a pool of blood than a banana skin. This comedic edge threatens to drag the film into the ridiculous but the narrative is kept believ-able by the intense straight performances of the four leads.

Ken Foree as Peter makes a compassionate hero, haunted by the killing but still strong and capable. David Emge also excels as the weakest, most ordinary of the three males. He plays Stephen with a human fallibility, idolising Peter like a kid brother and becoming obsessed by the mall's offerings. When the biker looters turn up, despite Peter's warnings Stephen decides to stay and shoot it out. 'It's ours,' he cries. 'We took it.' The decision ends up costing him more than just his life.

As Fran, Gaylen Ross is another of Romero's resolute females. She begins as Stephen's nagging girlfriend – 'I would have made you all coffee and breakfast but I forgot my pots and pans' – and snipes at being left behind as the boys explore the mall. By the film's conclusion she's found strength, learnt to shoot better than Stephen and fly a helicopter without assistance. With a new life growing in her belly, she's the next best hope for the future of mankind. With this mixture of horror, comedy and humanity Romero has created a masterpiece. *Dawn of the Dead* is simply the final word on the zombie subgenre: gaudy, over-the-top and a film of splattering originality.

American Nightmare: The horror of the Vietnam War and the political mistrust that spread in the aftermath of Watergate left Americans feeling impudent. Sure, the world was corrupt but what could you do about it? Apathy was quick to take hold and society looked for distractions elsewhere. In the 1970s, shopping became America's favourite pastime and the mall was the perfect hiding place from injustice. In *Dawn* the group turn it into a luxurious utopia. They eat the best foods (caviar, cheeses, fresh bread), drink the best wine, turn their living quarters into a bourgeois home and wander around in expensive fur coats and shiny watches.

Yet they are clinging to normality in the most artificial place on Earth. They can go nowhere in their new clothes, do nothing but drink bottle after bottle of wine and remain virtual prisoners within their decadent home. The group become bored and distant, Stephen and Fran barely able to speak without bickering. At night they lie naked in bed together, both still, staring vacantly into space like two shop-window dummies. The world is theirs and it is stifling. On the roof, Peter, decked out in lavish tracksuit bottoms, plays squash against the wall. As he leaves, he knocks a tennis ball down off the roof and on to the car park below. The undead inhabit it like a swarm of locusts, a grim reminder of the horror that dominates the outside world. Inside, the group continue to ignore the problem – and will do so until it crashes in through the front door. For Romero, the mall is representative of America itself.

From the Vault: In 2007, an annual two-day festival kicked off in the UK dedicated to Ken Foree. ForeeFest features an appearance by the man himself, special guests, Q & As, signings and screenings of his movies.

Undead or Alive: *Dawn of the Dead* is the one he'll be remembered for – a beautiful walking corpse of a movie that dug its broken fingernails deep into the heart of American culture. To this day it refuses to let go. Definitive. 5/5

Knightriders (1981)
Camelot is a state of mind.

Crew: Director/Writer: George A. Romero, Producer: Richard P. Rubinstein, Cinematographer: Michael Gornick, Editors: Pasquale Buba and George A. Romero, Production Designer: Cletus Anderson, Composer: Donald Rubinstein

Cast: Ed Harris (Billy), Gary Lahti (Alan), Tom Savini (Morgan), Amy Ingersoll (Linet), Christine Forrest (Angie), Brother Blue

(Merlin), John Amplas (Whiteface), Martin Ferrero (Bontempi),
Ken Foree (Little John), Scott Reiniger (Marhalt)
146 mins

Working Title: *Knights*

Ripping Yarn: Fight or yield? An Arthurian renaissance fair
travels America, stopping in small towns, selling medieval bric-
a-brac and performing death-defying battles. Only these knights
don't ride on horseback – they duel on motorcycles. Billy, the
king of this makeshift Camelot, is plagued by nightmares of a
huge black bird. He's been battered in a series of violent jousts
and Morgan, the leader of the Black Knights, has his eye on
the throne.

In a redneck town the troupe play to a drunken and cynical
crowd and an obese local cop threatens to shut them down
unless he gets paid off. Billy refuses. For him this is more than
just a living; it's a way of life. He lives by a code of honour
and expects the same from his followers. Later on the cop
returns and throws Billy and his friend Bagman in jail. In his
absence the group begin to question Billy's almost fascistic
idealism and their own hand-to-mouth existence.

Moving on to the next town the knights are approached
by Joe Bontempi ('good times in Italian!'), a sleazy agent who
offers to take them into the big time. Morgan is tempted and
Billy returns to find the group pulling apart. That afternoon's
joust falls into chaos when a gang of bikers show up in their
own armour. Billy stands to fight and comes face to face with
a Native American knight. He wears on his chest plate the
painting of a huge black bird...

Making a Monster: From an early age Romero loved the
legend of King Arthur: the knights, the magic and the nobility.

Even as an adult he reread T.H. White's Arthurian saga *The Once and Future King* whenever he could. In 1976 he planned to direct a medieval epic, only with the romance gone and the knights infected and syphilitic – a period movie from down in the mud. He pitched the idea to Samuel Z. Arkoff (head of American International Pictures and the producer of motorcycle quickies like *The Wild Angels* [1966]). Arkoff was unconvinced. 'Maybe I should put the knights on motorcycles and add a rock 'n' roll soundtrack!'[9] mocked Romero. Somehow the idea stuck.

Inspired by real-life renaissance fair The Society for Creative Anachronism, Romero set about transporting his tale of gallant knights into the modern world. But even with this switch in time period *Knights*, as it was then known, was a hard sell and it wasn't until the massive commercial success of *Dawn of the Dead* that Romero was able to secure the necessary \$3.7 million budget. A sizable chunk of this would go on the motorcycle sequences, and producer Richard Rubinstein hired Stunts Incorporated, the famous team behind *Smokey and the Bandit* (1977), to get the job done. They had set new standards in automotive acrobatics and had the bruises to prove it. Supervisor Gary Davis showed up on set in a full body cast, which didn't get removed until the first day of production. They subsequently got through over 60 bikes, leaving pieces of twisted metal everywhere.

For the most part *Knightriders* was shot at a Lodge just outside Pittsburgh. The place was the usual haunt of the local gun club, whose members consisted mainly of trigger-happy 'good ol' boys', and the African Americans on set were not welcome. Further problems blighted the shoot when the weather turned hostile and a tornado destroyed most of the set. Out of 96 shooting days, 82 were hit by rain. In the face of these adversities the cast and crew began to form a deep bond. 'We became that troupe,' explained Romero. 'We weren't going to be beaten.'[10]

Knightriders was released in 1981 and went head to head with *Excalibur*, John Boorman's more traditional take on the Arthurian legend. Both films failed to meet audience expectations but, while Boorman's film managed respectable business, *Knightriders* bombed spectacularly. On the upside, the film featured a cameo from bestselling author Stephen King, and whilst on set he handed Romero a copy of his new book *The Stand* with an inscription inside reading 'Maybe we'll make this together someday'. They never did, but instead teamed up to make something altogether creepier...

Face of Death: In keeping with the medieval romance of the narrative, *Knightriders* adopts the classical veneer of European Renaissance painting. Like John William Waterhouse's *The Lady of Shalott* or Edmund Blair Leighton's *The Accolade* the film inhabits golden-brown forests, captures armour shimmering in the sunlight and dwells in the early-morning mist before battle. The heroic wonder of the knights is set in sharp contrast with the 'sucker-head American driftwood' that attends their shows. Billy is square jawed and broad shouldered. The audience are slobbish and rotund; wearing sweat-stained Hawaiian shirts and spraying food from their thick mouths. It is clear which way of life Romero prefers.

The motorcycle jousts are jaw dropping: fast paced and crunching as bikes fly through the air and flip over in slow motion. Maces clang down against rattling armour, lances splinter into a thousand pieces and loose gravel sprays under spinning tires. Michael Gornick's camera gets inches away from the action and we can feel every pounding blow and smell the gasoline pouring out from revving engines. In Billy's final battle, the Black Bird knight emerges through a cloud of dust and the two warriors ride with unbridled ferocity. Billy is victorious but badly wounded, and staggers across to his fallen adversary. He places the point of his sword on the knight's battered chest and the camera follows a trickle of blood down Billy's arm, along his blade and on to the Black Bird. *Knightriders* is a visually exquisite piece of cinema.

Digging up the Dead: Billy has created his own functioning society outside the mainstream. His companions have become like family and they live their own way. Life is a constant struggle, but the need to resist the compromise offered by Bontempi is vital in maintaining this alternative way of life. *Knightriders* presents its nomadic group in idyllic fashion. They are good, hearty people who live a life of worth, selling hand-crafted artefacts and using the profits only as means of sustaining their lifestyle. The troupe are welcoming to other outsiders: 'You take in every longhair who knows how to make a pair of sandals,' lawyer Steve tells Billy.

However Romero is aware of the pitfalls of this existence. Morgan is lured away by the promise of easy money (and easier women) and Billy has become despotic in his bid to hang on to the life. We first meet him self-flagellating in a river and later watch as he rants about 'fighting the dragon' of consumerism. He denies a kid his autograph and screams at his troupe, 'Nobody goes anywhere in this outfit without my permission!' Ed Harris, in his breakthrough role, is perfect, playing the role with Aryan intensity: 'The code that we're living is the truth,' he states. 'The truth is the code.'

Though cautious of Billy's zealot mania, Romero clearly identifies with him, and in some respects looks up to him. He takes Billy's talk of destiny ('the big D' as the scatting-hip-hop Merlin puts it) seriously and as a result the film lapses into pretension. With the exception of Tom Savini's masterful interpretation of the rogue knight Morgan – torn between self and the group ('I gotta love myself,' he explains. 'Everyone else thinks I'm an asshole.') – the rest of the cast has a tendency to appear over earnest, merely there to spout Romero's unusually wet dialogue. 'You give us everything,' one follower tells Billy. 'You give us a chance.'

The film's epic running length is at least 30 minutes too long, making viewing a hard slog. Billy's final, po-faced motorcycle ride towards destiny could be cut and the numerous subplots, like Alan's trip to see hippie friends, could also be lost without much damage. But *Knightriders* is far from a total failure and contains a fascinating autobiographical overtone. In his career, George A. Romero created his own functioning production company outside the mainstream. His companions became like family and they made movies their own way. Life is a struggle, but the need to resist the compromise offered by Hollywood is vital in maintaining his unique brand of cinema. This isn't a film about knights, it's about George Romero.

American Nightmare: Whereas almost all of Romero's movies point towards a dysfunctional America, *Knightriders* was the first to offer a tangible alternative. Billy's group comprises disparate outsiders shunned by ordinary society. They are America's unwanted: strong women, blacks, ethnics, dwarves, homosexuals, atheists. They have fought hard to create a separate life where they can live equally and free of judgement – a place where they can belong. Tourney announcer Pip is struggling with his own sexuality but is faced with no antagonism from the surrounding performers. They simply push him to except who he is, something they all did long ago.

This slightly naïve slant to the film didn't mean the director was any less angry. In the 1980s the 'greed is good' mantra was becoming the code most Americans lived by. For Romero, capitalistic want is corrupting, and here it is the one thing that threatens to pull the group apart. 'You can keep the money you make off this sick world,' rages Billy. 'I don't want any part of it.' But Morgan and his Black Knights are seduced by the almighty dollar, leaving the troupe for a new life of decadence and swimming pools. In this world, however, they are simply commodities used to sell tickets. Morgan is exploited and paraded around in a ridiculous jewelled codpiece to advertise fights. The film ends with him returning to the group and facing up to his responsibilities to the way of life. 'You know those contracts?' he says to Bontempi. 'Burn 'em, baby.'

From the Vault: The role of the jive-talking Merlin was originally offered to a young Morgan Freeman. Freeman rejected the role, claiming lines like 'Magic got to do with the soul, man' were racist. The script's liberal themes and demand for equality were clearly lost on him.

Undead or Alive: The anachronistic visuals, spectacular bike stunts and the autobiographical themes make *Knightriders* a significant entry in the Romero canon. However, the film is also ponderous, slow and a little too worthy. Not a film just for Romero purists – but very nearly. 2/5

Creepshow (1982)
The most fun you'll ever have being scared.

Crew: Director: George A. Romero, Producer: Richard P. Rubinstein, Writer: Stephen King, Cinematographer: Michael Gornick, Editors: Pasquale Buba, Paul Hirsch, George A. Romero & Michael Spolan, Production Designer: Cletus

Anderson, Composer: John Harrison, Special Make-Up Effects:
Tom Savini

Cast: Hal Holbrook (Henry Northrup), Adrienne Barbeau
(Wilma Northrup), Fritz Weaver (Dexter Stanley), Leslie Nielsen
(Richard Vickers), E.G. Marshall (Upson Pratt), Viveca Lindfors
(Aunt Bedelia), Ed Harris (Hank Blaine), Ted Danson (Harry
Wentworth), Stephen King (Jordy Verrill)
115 mins

Original Title: *The Creep Show*

Ripping Yarn: Heh, heh! Welcome, kiddies, to five jolting
tales of horror. The first slice is entitled *Father's Day*. Rumour
has it Aunt Bedelia creamed her daddy on his special day –
just before serving his cake. But on the seventh anniversary
of his death the old man's spongy corpse rises looking for
some just desserts.

Not your piece of cake? Then *The Lonesome Death of Jordy
Verrill* is sure to grow on you. A glowing meteor crashes into
a field, covering everything in a weird alien plant life – even
poor old Jordy. He's gonna find out the grass isn't always
greener on the other side.

In *Something to Tide You Over* Rebecca's affair with Harry
doesn't wash with husband Richard. The tide's coming in and
the loving couple soon find themselves up to their necks in
it.

If the previous yarn was too deep, then *The Crate* should
keep you boxed in. When a college janitor opens an ancient
coffer, he lets loose a bloodthirsty monster. It nearly sends
Dexter Stanley off his casket, but his buddy Henry sees the
opportunity to get something off his chest – namely his nagging
wife Billie.

Bugged yet? If not, the final skin-crawling tale will do the trick. In *They're Creeping up on You*, Upson Pratt's expensive germ-proof penthouse is overrun with cockroaches. This time it's not just the landlord who's making a pest of himself. Spray it! Squash it! Kill it!

That's all for this time, kiddies. Stay scared! Heh, heh!

Making a Monster: Ahem. Romero first met Stephen King back in 1976 when Warner Brothers' executives where adapting King's vampire novel *Salem's Lot* into a movie. Figuring the *Martin* director would be perfect for the project, the pair were introduced. Sadly, *Lot* was eventually considered too expensive for the big screen, but they remained eager to work together. King's *The Stand* seemed perfect.

The novel's story concerning plague and global apocalypse was epic and any film adaptation would have demanded a budget of at least $20 million. With King having no track record as a screenwriter and Romero hardly a box-office cert, they decided to make a low-budget horror movie to prove themselves – a sort of tune-up project. Almost simultaneously they struck upon the idea of a horror anthology in the vein of *Dr Terror's House of Horrors* (1964). King wanted to do a *Monty Python*-style sketch show, with punch lines of gore rather than jokes. Romero thought each segment should trace the history of horror: one shot in black and white, one in 3-D, one in widescreen. Somewhere in between they found *Creepshow*.

King shared Romero's childhood love of William Gaines' EC Comics and was enthusiastic to turn *Creepshow* into a full-blooded tribute. It took him only 60 days to write the screenplay, with *The Lonesome Death of Jordy Verrill* and *The Crate* based on stories he'd already published. Romero was so impressed he decided to shoot the first draft and, with $8 million secured from UFD, the film went into production in the spring of 1981. It was the biggest budget Romero had worked with thus far in his career.

This increased funding saw Romero opt for name actors – another first – and Hal Holbrook (*All the President's Men* [1976]), E.G. Marshall (*Twelve Angry Men* [1957]), Tom Atkins and Adrienne Barbeau (both from John Carpenter's *The Fog* [1979]) and Leslie Nielson (*Airplane!* [1980]) all took part. With most of the names appearing in different segments, Romero felt like he was directing five episodes of *Columbo*, each with a different guest star. The movie's other performers were the 18,000 cockroaches needed for *They're Creeping up on You*. On set they were uncontrollable – living and breeding everywhere. If Pittsburgh later had a 'roach epidemic, then it was probably Romero's fault.

Following a midnight screening at Cannes in 1982, the film was ironically picked up by Warner Brothers for distribution. They secured Romero his first ever number one at the US box office and a $25 million return to go with it. *The New York Post* proclaimed that 'for kids from 6 to 60 who never want to grow up, this is a most bewitching brew'.[11] Unfortunately, the film's goofy, comic-strip vibe wasn't taken seriously by studios and *Creepshow* did nothing to raise King and Romero's industry credibility. Based on this movie, *The Stand* would never get made – at least not by Romero.

Face of Death: 'A great part of my aesthetic in the genre was born out of EC rather than movies,'[12] explained Romero. Both *The Crazies* and *Dawn of the Dead* had toyed with the exaggerated colours of those early comics, but *Creepshow* was a full-on assimilation. The stories come from a kid's comic book and the static camera, obscure angles and multicoloured texture resembles living comic panels. Shots are on a severe tilt and dissolves are achieved by the turning of a page. The monsters too are fittingly baroque, from the dead dad in *Father's Day* – with maggots in his eye sockets and white slime dripping from his teeth – to the drowned couple in *Something to Tide You Over* with their wrinkled blue skin and seaweed hair.

The lighting is full of bold green and blue gels and turns blood red whenever something grisly happens (like when the beast in *The Crate* chews up the janitor). So extreme were these techniques that lab technicians processing the film thought there'd been an error and corrected all the footage to look normal. It had to be reshot. In between segments the film actually transforms into a comic book (drawn by Rick Catizone) and, as the pages turn to the next story, we see readers' letters and adverts for x-ray glasses and voodoo dolls. *Creepshow* is a visual treat that even now is being imitated in such big-budget productions as Ang Lee's *Hulk* (2003) and Robert Rodriguez's *Sin City* (2005).

The Splatter Factor: Tom Savini was getting a reputation. Due to his previous work with Romero and some inventive butchering on *Friday the 13th* (1980) the industry began to see him as a kind of splatter savant. Savini, however, wanted something more than just latex appliances and fake blood. Like Dr Frankenstein, he wanted to make monsters.

To introduce the movie Romero wanted a skeletal spectre; the kind of thing reminiscent of the Crypt Keeper from *Tales from the Crypt*. Rather than build make-up on to an actor, Savini dug up (not literally) a real skeleton and transformed it into the floating ghoul known as The Creep. The skull was completely animatronic, with rolling eyes and a jaw that could laugh hysterically. It took eight people to operate, but only two to build – Savini and his 17-year-old apprentice worked alone.

Their biggest challenge was constructing 'Fluffy', the Tasmanian devil that runs amok in *The Crate*. The screenplay description was vague – 'we see a blur of fur and teeth' – so Savini invented it from scratch. Having no experience in creature animatronics, he called Rob Bottin, the effects genius behind *The Howling* (1980). Bottin gave step-by-step instructions, leading Savini to create a matt-haired, salivating, knife-toothed work of art. *Creepshow* finally elevated Savini to the level of effects contemporaries Rick Baker (of *An American Werewolf in London* [1981]) and *Dead and Buried*'s (1981) Stan Winston. But it was his next film for Romero that would leave them behind in his bloody wake.

Digging up the Dead: *Creepshow* is a love letter, a joyous homage to the comic-book monsters King and Romero devoured as kids. They have captured the feel perfectly and everything about the movie screams EC. When Robin Wood chastised it for showing 'nasty people doing nasty things to other nasty people'[13] he was right – except that he saw this as a bad thing. Though grizzly, EC comics contained a strong, if basic, moral code. The message to kids was simple: do something bad and something bad will happen to you.

The comic delighted in showing the worst kinds of deviants getting their comeuppance and the movie loyally follows suit. In *Something to Tide You Over* Richard is a sadist and a torturer. He films his acts and, after burying his wife and her lover in sand, later watches the footage back as they drown in the tide. By the story's conclusion Richard has ended up in their place, screaming manically, 'I can hold my breath for a long time!' For his sins he's going to have to. All the nasty characters meet their fate with a similar, ironic form of karma. You better behave, says Romero, or the bogyman's gonna getcha.

Aside from dark kismet, the movie also borrows the comic's

illicit edge. As a kid Romero had to read EC comics in secret, away from his disapproving parents. So did King. For younger horror fans, *Creepshow* has the same effect, something to watch with the sound low and one finger on the off button when your parents have gone to bed. The film is full of excessive horror: a hairy creature claws wet chunks out of a grad student's neck; bugs crawl out of a dead billionaire's mouth. King's screenplay, too, is deliriously profane. 'I'll be dipped in shit if that ain't a meteor!' Jordy Verrill exclaims at what's glowing in his field. Later, in *The Crate*, Billie is equally expressive when confronting her murderous husband: 'Get out of my way, Henry, or I swear to God you'll be wearing your balls as earrings.' It makes the 12 year old in you chuckle every time.

In front of the camera, big names Holbrook, Marshall and Neilson are near perfect, but it's the less established actors who get the best out of the two-dimensional characters. Adrienne Barbeau is a booze-sodden bitch, belittling her husband in public and talking like a hyena on crack: 'Just call me Billie. Everyone does.' You can sort of understand why he wants to feed her to a monster. Amazingly, non-actor Stephen King steals the film. Buck toothed and bug eyed as the hard-on-his-luck Jordy Verrill, King is a walking Looney Toon. 'Oh, Jordy, you lunkhead,' he mutters at himself. His performance is gormless, gruesome and genuinely fun to be around – much like the film itself.

From the Vault: The kid secretly reading horror comics in his bedroom (and who later voodoos poor Tom Atkins to death) is Joe King, the real-life son of the film's writer. Today Joe has followed in his dad's footsteps and become a novelist in his own right.

Undead or Alive: *Creepshow* achieves what it set out to do and it is, as Stephen King stated, basically 'a junk-food movie'.[14] It may be junk food, but it's prepared with love. 4/5

Day of the Dead (1985)
The darkest day of horror the world has ever known.

Crew: Director/Writer: George A. Romero, Producer: Richard P. Rubinstein, Cinematographer: Michael Gornick, Editor: Pasquale Buba, Production Designer: Cletus Anderson, Composer: John Harrison, Special Make-Up Effects: Tom Savini

Cast: Lori Cardille (Sarah), Terry Alexander (John), Joe Pilato (Rhodes), Jarlath Conroy (McDermott), G. Howard Klar (Steel), John Amplas (Fisher), Richard Liberty (Dr Logan), Howard Sherman (Bub)
101 mins

Ripping Yarn: The dead now outnumber the living by four hundred thousand to one. The cities are devoid of life, the power is off and 'all the shopping malls are closed'. The moans of the living dead fill the city skies. In an underground military complex a group of scientists led by Dr Logan (Frankenstein to everyone else) and Sarah work on ending the zombie epidemic. Specimens are kept in a corral not far from where they sleep.

Following the death of Major Cooper, the tyrannical Captain Rhodes has taken charge. During a meeting tensions rise and, when the soldiers become aggressive, Sarah decides to walk out. Rhodes gives her a choice: 'Sit down or, so help me God, I'll have you shot.' Living 24 hours in this lifeless cave is taking its toll. Only helicopter pilot John and technician McDermott seem completely sane, setting up camp away from the others and relaxing with the odd glass of brandy.

Sarah's lover Miguel is becoming hysterical. After a botched attempt to gather specimens he is bitten and Sarah attempts to save him by chopping off his infected arm. But Miguel is no longer thinking about life. Meanwhile Dr Logan has stopped searching for a cure and is now after ways to control the dead. His 'star pupil', Bub, is a zombie with signs of intelligence – but only on the promise of a reward to come. He could be humanity's only hope…

Making a Monster: *Old Soldiers Never Die – Satan Sends them Back* was the title of Romero's treatment for his third and (at the time) final zombie movie. The concluding chapter was to be monumental, an explosive epic with zombie soldiers and gung-ho rebels – more *Raiders of the Lost Ark* (1981) than *Night of the Living Dead*. With a budget of around $7 million needed, financiers UFD demanded an R rating. Either that or Romero could deliver an unrated version for half that amount. The director couldn't see a *Dead* picture without the gruel and, with a heavy heart, decided to take the $3.5 million.

The final script was a pared-down version of the original. Characters such as Rhodes, Sarah and John remained, while others were cut entirely. The gigantic scale was also reduced and the action now mainly took place in the underground complex. For this location the production discovered a 125-acre limestone mine in Wampum, Pennsylvania, a place used to store everything from government records to millionaires' yachts. Shooting began in October 1984 with days beginning at seven and running through till eight at night. The cast and crew didn't see daylight for almost three months and as a result were plagued by sickness. The limestone dust didn't help either. 'When you blew your nose… there was black dust in your handkerchief,' [15] explained Tom Savini.

The role of Sarah went to New York stage actress Lori Cardille, a Pittsburgher whose dad 'Chilly Billy' had appeared in *Night*. Dr Logan was written specifically for *The Crazies* actor Richard Liberty and Howard Sherman, a theatre actor and sometime mime, got the role of Bub after auditioning while chomping on a turkey leg. Romero regulars Joe Pilato (*Knightriders*), Antoné DiLeo (also *Knightriders*) and John Amplas (*Martin*) filled out the supporting roles. As usual, Romero generated a relaxed atmosphere on set and allowed his actors to improvise. The now iconic sequence where Logan gives Bub a walkman ('I… ain't… finished') was created by the two performers.

Released in July 1985, *Day of the Dead* earned a respectable $1.7 million in its opening weekend. This quickly dropped off, mainly due to competition from zombie comedy *Return of the Living Dead* (which many mistook for a Romero picture). Fans had hoped *Day* would contain a similar knockabout style to *Dawn* and were disappointed by the overall gloomy tone. Critic Dean Levi went as far as to call it 'a cesspool of vile filth produced by a sick mind for sick-minded people'.[16] Clearly not a Romero fan.

But at the time the Pittsburgh-based filmmaker was also unhappy with the result. The film was far from the definitive sign out to zombie cinema that he had intended. He had proceeded with production due to contractual obligations with UFD and an eagerness to end his partnership with Richard Rubinstein. *Day of the Dead* was a fine movie but left fans, and Romero himself, wanting more. Twenty years later, Romero's zombies would rise again.

Face of Death: To emphasise *Day of the Dead*'s despairing tone, Romero and cinematographer Michael Gornick created a film that is visually more oppressive than both *Night* and *Dawn* combined. The film's labyrinth underground setting is a claustrophobic hell where you can almost smell the stale damp. There are no windows to let in natural light, the vast caverns lead only into empty blackness and the dim low-watt bulbs strung across the ceiling only serve to highlight the gloom. The only colour this place sees is the omnipresent khaki green of the soldiers' uniforms and, of course, the splattering of red blood. Their underground sanctuary is really, as John says, 'a 14-mile tombstone'.

Above ground things are no better. The deserted Florida landscape reveals a city beyond repair – beyond hope. Rusted cars litter the streets, useless money drifts in the air, buildings are derelict and torn newspapers reading 'THE DEAD WALK!' circulate in the dusty wind. The zombies here are more decayed and brittle, but at least dressed for the Florida sun – stumbling around in straw hats and Hawaiian shirts. Civilisation is finished. Cletus Anderson's beautifully realised matte paintings add scale to the scenes of Armageddon. Here the destruction seems to go on for miles, stretching out beyond view and into America.

The Splatter Factor: In a makeshift lab amidst pounding rock music, empty cans of soda and copies of *Fangoria* magazine, a group of lunatics are working hard to make George Romero's nightmares come true. They throw together severed limbs, sloppy bite wounds and a whole bucketful of gooey effects, all under the instruction of one man. After all, this is the place they call 'Saviniland'.

On *Day of the Dead* Tom Savini surpassed himself. Openly collaborating with a large team of SFX artists – Howard

Berger, John Vulich and Greg Nicotero (affectionately known as 'Gut Boy' because, well, he was in charge of the guts) – Savini created some of the finest terror-filled illusions ever committed to celluloid. From the faceless zombie on the medical slab with his brain exposed, to the screaming soldier having his head pulled off by hungry zombies, these effects, even today, defy belief.

The make-up itself was a vast improvement on *Dawn*'s grey-painted zombies, with the undead fitted with prosthetic appliances and facial disfigurements. Whilst latex was used in abundance, human insides were replicated using real animal guts. When somebody turned off the freezer containing these bloody insides, actor Joe Pilato was forced to film his death scene chest deep in rancid entrails. Regardless, the finished film, along with perhaps Rob Bottin's work on *The Thing* (1982), represented a high point for special make-up effects. Savini regards it as his masterpiece. It's hard to disagree.

Digging up the Dead: The $7 million version of *Day of the Dead* ranks alongside Orson Welles' *Don Quixote* and Richard Donner's *Superman 2* as one of cinema's great lost projects. Romero's 204-page screenplay is available online for fans wishing to daydream about what might have been, but, this said, the finished film is not without value. The director's frustration has smothered *Day* in a bitter anger and, as a result, it is the darkest of the saga. This is a film about the end of the world – and Romero seems glad.

Sarah searches for ways to return civilisation back to normal, but John views it as a waste of time. The 'normal' society represented by Rhodes and his men is racist (Miguel is dismissed as a 'yellow son of a bitch') and violent (when there are no zombies to shoot they pound on each other after lights out). To John the zombies are a religious plague, ravaging the land of sin. 'We are being punished by the creator,' he tells Sarah. Eventually, and seemingly deservedly, the old society is ripped to pieces.

This pessimistic tone is rendered all the more fractious by the enclosed space of the complex. In this hellishly reversed world the dead walk the streets above while the living are buried in the ground below. The central performances have been accused of being too big, but seem in keeping with men driven to the edge by death and cabin fever. The soldiers are like dogs locked in a hot car with the windows rolled up. 'I'm running this monkey farm now, Frankenstein!' barks Captain Rhodes with foam virtually bubbling from his mouth. And as the soldiers become more irrational and Rhodes executes a doctor in cold blood, it becomes clear that the living are now more dangerous than the undead. 'He's human,' observes John of the captain. 'That's what scares me.'

Indeed, Romero's sympathies seem increasingly with the walking dead. As Dr Logan (in a blood-stained lab coat) disposes of specimens quickly with a drill bit through the cranium, we begin to pity them. Then there's Bub – the zombie with a soul. He's a wide-eyed innocent who curiously plays with objects given to him by Logan (a razor, a walkman and a copy of Stephen King's *Salem's Lot*). There are memories here. But the more human he becomes, the more dangerous he is. On seeing Captain Rhodes, Bub salutes and then remembers how to shoot a gun. It's only a matter of time before this dead soldier gets to use it.

The world of *Day of the Dead* is one of constant nightmares and Sarah dreams of zombie hands crashing through walls and her lover Miguel dripping out his insides. Even in sleep there is no respite from the horror and here Romero has produced an oppressive and claustrophobic masterpiece that stands shoulder-to-shoulder with its undead predecessors.

Never mind 'When there's no more room in hell...' This *is* hell.

American Nightmare: 'This is a fucking war!' yells Rhodes with an American flag hanging behind him. In the 1980s it seemed President Ronald Reagan was hoping for just that, actively heightening the Cold War with the Soviets and pouring billions of US dollars into his army. This was the largest peacetime military build up in world history. For Reagan, the Russians were virtual devils, reserving for themselves 'the right to commit any crime, to lie, to cheat, in order to obtain their ends'.[17] This was the politics of fear long before George W. stepped into the White House. Romero wasn't convinced. For him the military were dangerous; even more so when given total power. 'Anybody fucks with my command, they get court-martialled. They get executed,' Captain Rhodes tells Sarah.

In *Day*, the best hope for mankind lies not in the military or in government, but in America's outsiders. John is black, Sarah a strong independent woman and McDermott an Irish immigrant. Only they have the resources to escape the bunker and find a new way of life. Indeed, John's helicopter becomes a modern-day Noah's Ark carrying its minorities to the 'promised land'. In order to thrive they must abandon the old culture completely and teach their children 'never to come over here and dig these records out'. Romero's zombies, meanwhile, are a biblical flood – rising to wash away the hopeless old world in a river of human blood.

From the Vault: John Harrison's score was sampled in 2001 by UK band *The Gorillaz*. The track 'M1 A1' also contains the sound of *Day*'s Miguel screaming 'Hello! Hello! Is anyone there?' The group are big Romero fans and references to his movies crop up throughout their music.

Undead or Alive: Romero's third zombie film is not the disappointment fans and critics originally perceived it to be. With its evolution of the dead, grotesque terror and night-marish vision of the end of the world, *Day* stands up as not only a worthy entry in the saga, but also one of the most powerful horror movies of the 1980s. 5/5

Hollywood Horror Show

Things at Laurel began to turn sour. Looking for more econom-
ically viable business ventures, Rubinstein began to focus on
TV, namely the horror anthology series *Tales from the Darkside*.
Making films with Romero was fine, but the director was
more interested in personal vision than box office. Rubinstein
wanted stability, but Romero was still looking for anarchy.
Despite penning a number of scripts for the show, including
one about a cookie-making witch (*Baker's Dozen* from Season
Three), Romero was unhappy with this change in dynamic.
He found his directing projects getting pushed to one side
and in June 1985 decided to go freelance.

Rather than sever all ties, he continued to be associated
with Laurel as a director/writer for hire. He wrote the abysmal
Creepshow 2 (1987) and signed up to direct an adaptation of
Stephen King's *Pet Sematary*. After all, he liked it in Pittsburgh.
But, at the same time, the professional sheen of both *Creepshow*
and *Day of the Dead* left him with a newfound confidence and
he felt that he could finally take on Hollywood. 'I lost my
tendency to feel intimidated by the mainstream,' he stated at
the time. 'I learned I could co-exist with the grown-up world
out there, beyond the bend in the Ohio River.'[1] The regional
filmmaker finally decided to get himself an agent. Maybe
Hollywood wouldn't be that bad, he thought. He thought
wrong.

Monkey Shines (1988)
An Experiment in Fear.

Crew: Director/Writer: George A. Romero, Producer: Charles Evans, Cinematographer: James A. Contner, Editor: Pasquale Buba, Production Designer: Cletus Anderson, Composer: David Shire, Special Make-Up Effects: Tom Savini, Monkey Trainer: Alison Pascoe

Cast: Jason Beghe (Allan Mann), John Pankow (Geoffrey), Kate McNeil (Melanie), Joyce Van Patten (Dorothy Mann), Christine Forrest (Maryanne), Stanley Tucci (Dr John Wiseman), Boo (Ella)
108 mins

Alternative Title: *Ella*

Ripping Yarn: While out training, college track star and law student Allan Mann is hit by a truck. His spine is severely damaged and an operation by Dr John Wiseman fails to bring about a full recovery. Movement in Allan's head and neck is all that remains. His house is refitted for his needs and a nurse, Maryanne, moves in upstairs on constant call. Slowly Allan sinks into depression and attempts to suffocate himself in a polythene bag.

His best friend is worried. Geoffrey is a scientist experimenting on enhancing the intelligence of monkeys. Seeing Allan's constant need for help, he decides to give him his most developed specimen, Ella, to do the everyday chores Allan can't. Ella begins to revolutionise his life and becomes the hands and legs that he has lost. The two develop a deep connection.

But the drugs Geoffrey is still giving Ella are producing

weird side effects. Allan can somehow see through the monkey's eyes and, in turn, he becomes more animalistic. They become like one. At home he is frustrated by a bird Maryanne keeps and one night Ella strangles it. Later he learns that Dr Wiseman missed something during his surgery and that his paraplegia may be reversible. He is furious. After dark, full of Allan's rage, Ella slips out and heads for Wiseman's house. She is the primordial side of Allan's psyche made flesh and is ready to kill for him…

Making a Monster: Romero was on his own and, for the first time since 1973, without the backing of Richard Rubinstein. Perhaps lured by the opportunity to direct, both cinematographer Michael Gornick and composer John Harrison stayed with Laurel (Gornick helmed *Creepshow 2* while Harrison was behind 1991's *Tales from the Darkside: The Movie*). The family had broken up and Romero needed a project of his own.

Based on the novel by English writer Michael Stewart, *Monkey Shines* was being developed by *Tootsie* (1982) producer Charles Evans (brother of legendary Hollywood mogul Robert). Stewart had attempted the screenplay himself, but Romero came on board with his own ideas. 'I committed the sin everyone blames the studio for – I just took the things I liked and wrote the screenplay without any conscience.'[2] Though the completed script contained some noticeable changes – the Oxford University setting was switched to Pittsburgh and some minor characters were eliminated – the tone and overall themes remained the same.

The film was budgeted at $7 million and Orion Pictures stepped in to foot the bill. But to them, Romero was a maverick who needed watching. He was given a director of photography and overruled in casting. The role of the bitchy

Nurse Maryanne ('Why don't you do us all a favour and fill [Ella's] container with rat poison?') was written for his actress wife Christine, but Evans and Orion insisted she be auditioned. They wanted a say in everything.

Ella was provided by Helping Hands, a real-life organisation that trains monkeys to assist paraplegics. Much of the crew's efforts involved coaxing a performance out of the film's simian star and Romero and the crew would dance around in Mexican hats and wave maracas to get the appropriate reactions. When Ella needed to be affectionate with Allan, they'd have to wait for her to be in heat.

Romero regular Pasquale Buba was responsible for editing and made a cut ready for audience previews. This was Romero's first experience of the process, where a random group of people are grabbed off the street, made to watch the movie and then asked what they did or didn't like. Hollywood producers have been known to live or die by the results. The audience didn't like the ending, where Allan, as in the novel, ends the film happy but still paralysed and Dean Burbage continues Geoffrey's experiments, so Orion and Evans politely pressurised Romero to change it.

The new ending sees Allan miraculously walk and also contains a *Carrie*-inspired dream sequence where a monkey claws out of his back during surgery. Romero had fulfilled his contractual obligation, but he was far from happy. Despite fine reviews the film failed to gain its money back at the box office and Orion's own financial troubles meant it wouldn't be seen in the UK for nearly two years. His first film for a major Hollywood studio had seen him compromised and questioned at every turn. It was just the start of his problems.

Face of Death: With a Hollywood budget and an experienced cameraman at his disposal, Romero went for broke with a glossy and uninhibited visual style unlike anything he'd shot before. The top-of-the-line camera equipment, the studio settings and the professionals who surrounded him left him free to experiment. He was like a kid in a toy store playing with an expensive train set. His camera charges across rooms attached to Allan's wheelchair, pans and tracks with balletic grace, and, in POV shots of Ella the monkey, it literally climbs out the window, down a tree and leaps through the back garden.

As usual, Romero's set pieces are expertly staged, only now with an added flourish. In the film's climax, with Allan and Melanie falling in love, Ella becomes jealous and attempts to win back his affection by electrocuting his overbearing mother. Lightning crashes outside and inside the lights fuse, leaving them in the stormy darkness. When Melanie shows up, Ella springs at her clutching a razorblade and, as she falls, the camera rises into the air and spins around and around watching Ella slash at her face. This from a director who, in the past, was reluctant to even take the camera off the tripod.

The Splatter Factor: Unlike the showy and upfront splatter of *Day of the Dead*, this film required something subtler and demanded fewer gross-out effects. Savini and his team's main role was to build stunt monkeys. The real simian actors were unreliable so Savini built a full-sized replica out of foam rubber, which could be flipped around on the end of a fishing wire to make it look like it was really jumping. Once covered in hair the end result was remarkably lifelike. Savini was proving himself to be adept at more that just splatter.

For Ella's close ups the team got to work on an animatronic version, lovingly referred to as 'Robochimp'. The real monkeys wouldn't stop moving, so 'Robo' was brought in for shots where Ella had to be still and listen to other characters speak. With his workload lighter than normal, Savini found time to relax on set and decided to parade around dressed as a demon warrior, complete with giant horns and full armour. It's a hell of an interesting way to make a living.

Digging up the Dead: Despite studio interference and the absence of his usual collaborators, with *Monkey Shines* Romero was still able to deliver a taut and genuinely thrilling horror picture. Much of Stewart's original novel remains and the allusion to man's repressed animalistic tendencies is fully explored in both novel and film. Allan's mental fusion with his pet helper brings out a more instinctive and feral side to him. He screams wildly at his friends and taunts Nurse Maryanne when her bird is found dead. 'Who gives a shit?' he sadistically hisses. 'It fucking deserved to die.'

Ella becomes the physical manifestation of this rage – the Mr Hyde to his Dr Jekyll (a theme that would later reappear in both *The Dark Half* and *Bruiser*). She kills for him without the burden of human morality and burns both the girlfriend who left him and doctor who botched his operation. Romero adds another layer of unease with an Oedipal relationship between Allan and his overbearing mother. As she bathes his naked body she expresses jealousy over his relationship with 'that Melanie girl'. Later, Allan lets loose, condemning her as a 'conniving, clinging, bloodsucking bitch', and she slaps the only part of his body that still has feeling. This act dooms her to become another of Allan/Ella's victims.

Allan's disability is also a source of terror. He is helpless when Ella attacks and can only sit there motionless when she turns on him; pissing on his lap and holding a blade up to his eye. There is also a workaday horror to the apparatus Allan needs to accommodate him: the metal cage that is his bed, the hoist that hangs from his ceiling like some medieval torture device. At the same time, the film treats him with respect and Allan is never caricatured as one of Hollywood's loveable disabled (see Dustin Hoffman in 1988's *Rain Man*). In his inability to control his own rages he is as much the cause of the film's antagonism as he is the victim.

The casting is a triumph and, although littered with unknowns, it is arguably Romero's finest line up. As Geoffrey, John Pankow is a revelation, somehow managing to make the mad, slightly unethical scientist both likeable and believable. He plays Geoffrey as a man driven by science, his eyes red and bleary, his face pale as he injects himself with a cocktail of drugs to keep him working over 24 hours. Jason Beghe also excels as Allan who, despite his character's slide into ranting mania, retains our sympathies. So much so that he even makes the tacked-on happy ending easy to swallow, and the fact that we like him and Melanie so much means we're happy to see him walk off into the sunset. Looking back, Romero may find the movie hard to watch, but, behind the studio meddlings, it shines.

American Nightmare: The focus on character over the director's usual social comment makes *Monkey Shines*, along with *The Dark Half*, one of his least politicised films. However, within Michael Stewart's original novel there is a strong anti-vivisection feel and Romero happily picks up on this. Dean Burbage's strong belief in the killing of research subjects is seen as damaging to the credibility of his work: 'I've seen you on three different talk shows defending the slaughter of animals,' yells Geoffrey. 'Your knife work has the anti-vivisectionists ready to firebomb the college.' They debate ferociously over the merits of the 'carrot or the stick' approach to animal testing but it becomes clear whose side Romero is on when we enter Burbage's lab – a grotesque torture chamber of drowning rats, metal slabs and bloodied white sheets. He's the real-life equivalent of *Day's* Dr Logan, and all the more terrifying for that.

From the Vault: In 1988 Romero should have begun work on Laurel's adaptation of Stephen King's *Pet Semetary*. When re-shoots for the ending of *Monkey Shines* delayed him, Rubinstein refused to wait and carried on the project with another director.

Undead or Alive: *Monkey Shines* is a fine entry into Romero's filmography and, despite studio interference, manages to stay true to the director's personality. Possibly the best killer-monkey film ever made. 4/5

Two Evil Eyes (1990)
When I wake you… you'll be dead.

Crew: Directors: George A. Romero & Dario Argento, Producers: Claudio & Dario Argento, Writers: George A. Romero, Dario Argento & Franco Ferrini, Cinematographers: Peter Reniers & Beppe Maccari, Editor: Pasquale Buba, Production Designer: Cletus Anderson, Composer: Pino Donaggio, Special Make-Up Effects: Tom Savini

Cast: Adrienne Barbeau (Jessica Valdemar), Ramy Zada (Dr Richard Hoffman), Bingo O'Malley (Ernest Valdemar), E.G. Marshall (Pike), Christine Forrest (Nurse), Tom Atkins (Cop), Harvey Keitel (Usher), Madeleine Potter (Annabel), Sally Kirkland (Eleonora), Kim Hunter (Mrs Pym), Martin Balsam (Mr Pym)
115 mins

Alternative Titles: *Edgar Allan Poe, Metropolitan Horrors, Due Occhi Diabolici* (Italian title)

Ripping Yarn: *The Facts in the Case of Mr Valdemar:* Wealthy businessman Ernest Valdemar is dying. His trophy wife Jessica is ravenous for his fortune and, along with her doctor/lover Richard, hatches a plan to steal it all. While immobile in his bed, Valdemar is placed under hypnosis by Richard and induced to liquidise his assets and sign the cash over to Jessica. One night, still under a trance, Valdemar dies and his soul becomes trapped between this world and the next. In the darkness of the afterlife he is surrounded by the Others: shapeless dead things that want to live. Valdemar's corpse has one warning for his unfaithful wife: 'They're coming.'

The Black Cat: Rod Usher is a murder-scene photographer: 'My specialty is still life,' he tells Inspector LeGrand. When his girlfriend Annabel brings home a stray black cat, Usher takes an instant dislike to it and strangles the little beast – but not before photographing the event for the cover of his book *Metropolitan Horrors*. Annabel is distraught at the cat's disappearance and a guilt-ridden Usher slips into alcoholism and madness. When he finds another black cat identical to the one he killed he takes it home to please Annabel. But the stench of death is on him and all Usher has on his mind is murder.

Making a Monster: Although Dario Argento's movies did well in Europe, American audiences were still relatively unaware of the Italian maestro's work. Films such as *Deep Red* and *Suspiria* had a grand, operatic bravado that preferred sensational set pieces to cohesive narrative. The Italians called it *giallo* (literally meaning yellow) after the yellow pulp novels with similar themes of grand murder. Looking to break into the American market, Argento determined to team up with several established US directors and produce a horror anthology – a sort of *Creepshow* for grown ups. He set his sights on John Carpenter (*Halloween* [1978]), Wes Craven (*A Nightmare on Elm Street* [1984]) and, of course, George A. Romero.

Argento's idea was to adapt four short stories by nine-teenth-century author Edgar Allan Poe, whose hallucinogenic fright tales had delighted him as a boy. Poe's stories had been adapted for the screen before, notably by Roger Corman in the 1960s, but Argento felt he and his collaborators could offer a fresh approach. Unfortunately, scheduling became a night-mare. With time restraints and other commitments looming, Craven and Carpenter dropped out, leaving just Dario and George to split the $9 million budget between them.

Argento planned to adapt Poe's *The Black Cat*, while Romero hoped to shoot *The Masque of the Red Death*. His version would be set in the future, where society has been ravaged by crime and an AIDS-style epidemic. A role was tailor written for Donald Sutherland who was already in talks to star as the narrator (possibly playing Poe himself). Argento and his producer brother Claudio hated it and sent Romero back to the drawing board. He returned with *The Facts in the Case of Mr Valdemar* and Argento was amused that Romero had chosen what he considered to be the only zombie story Poe ever wrote.

Shot in Pittsburgh during summer 1989, Argento and Romero gathered a stellar cast that included Harvey Keitel and *Creepshow* veterans Adrienne Barbeau, Tom Atkins and E.G. Marshall. The Italian director notoriously despised actors but somehow hit it off with Keitel. Overall, he had a good time. Romero was less fortunate. Having given up smoking (he took up the yo-yo to keep his hands busy), his nerves were fraught and lab errors with the film pushed the schedule back by five days. The piece was never close to his heart and, coupled with the problems on set, shooting felt like a chore.

Stateside, *Two Evil Eyes* received only a minimal release. Following the studio interference with *Monkey Shines* and his frustrations here, Romero seriously considered giving up directing for good. It would take a story by his old friend Stephen King to drag him back to the cinema.

Face of Death: Though Romero's chapter is unusually subdued, *Valdemar* still manages to produce some interesting stylistic turns. His locations are modern and ordinary (a high-rise apartment block, a Pittsburgh bank) but are also draped in a kind of Gothicism. Lightning crashes outside of arched windows, spiral staircases lead down into shadows and noises echo from out of the basement. Valdemar's mansion is functional, but also gloomy. Lit only by a few yellow lamps, it gives a sort of twentieth-century candlelight effect. Using contemporary appliances, Romero somehow draws out the billowing Victorian horror essential to Poe's writing.

With *The Black Cat* Argento is more kinetic and fast paced and, though less grandiose than, say, *Suspiria*, the segment contains flashes of baroque artistry. The camera swings back and forth on a lethal pendulum and follows a falling set of keys off a balcony and down on to the floor below – both moments that are uniquely Argento. His story is broader than *Valdemar*'s, taking in fiery medieval dreams and the coldness of downtown Pittsburgh. The constant shifts in location see Argento explore the city with the excitement of an outsider, hanging out in seedy bars and gazing up at the towering metropolis above him. It's a side of Pittsburgh rarely shown before, even by Romero.

The Splatter Factor: The effects in Romero's chapter were minimal. There was a squelchy death involving a pointed hypnosis device, some Valdemar zombie make-up and a frost-encrusted dummy corpse to be kept down in the cellar. But Tom Savini had done it all before. Sadly, he and Romero would fall out when Savini directed a remake of *Night of the Living Dead* and, though they have since repaired their friendship, the two would never work together as director/FX guru again. On this film, Savini had more fun with Argento. In *The Black Cat* there were bodies severed in two and rotten corpses half eaten and crammed in walls – stuff he could sink his teeth into.

Savini built replica black cats and (though it was never used in the finished film) a giant feline head for close ups. All the stops were pulled out for the film's final creature, when Usher buries his girlfriend behind a wall and accidentally traps the cat inside with her. The police are suspicious of Annabel's disappearance and, when searching Usher's house, hear meowing. They pull down the wall to find Annabel, dead, her face half eaten away. The black cat has had a litter. But they are mutated, mangy and furless; their wrinkled flesh like pink, uncooked turkey skin. They hiss, showing their razor teeth before continuing to feed on Annabel's clotted body.

Digging up the Dead: It is clear that, for both directors, *Two Evil Eyes* is a minor work, with the idea of their collaboration more interesting than the film itself. This said, these directors do know their way around a horror movie. Romero's segment is another of his morality tales while Argento's is typically perverse. Usher photographs scenes of graphic murder: a naked woman severed in two by a pendulum and another with her mouth clamped open and teeth pulled out by her lover cousin. These images are frank but also serve in pushing

Usher further towards madness. After all, how long can a man look into the abyss without the abyss looking back?

The murders in *The Black Cat* all relate to Poe (*The Pit and the Pendulum*, Poe's own marriage to his cousin) and Argento's film is a loving ode to his author hero. He glides through the writer's oeuvre and finds time to reference everything from *The Fall of the House of Usher* to *Annabel Lee*. In *Valdemar* Romero merely uses Poe as a starting point, expanding the writer's story to explore 1980s greed. On first viewing Adrienne Barbeau seems too old for the role of the trophy wife, but her increased age gives depth to a character that would otherwise be irredeemable. This is her last chance to obtain a comfortable life: 'I'm not society,' she tells lawyer Pike. 'I have nothing of my own.' It is desperation that lurks behind her heinous acts and Barbeau brings an inner vulnerability to the money-hungry bitch.

In *The Black Cat* Harvey Keitel is more unhinged. The madness that consumes him seems present from the start, with his opening narration dwelling on 'the depravity that is in us all'. The death he's witnessed through his camera lens has clearly disturbed him and the killing of the cat sends him over the edge. Usher is sweaty and paranoid, mumbling and dazed. 'You wanted to leave me, now we're together forever,' he says to his dead girlfriend before stuffing her body behind his upstairs wall.

The film's problem is length and both segments seem unnecessarily long. It's as if they were written to be around 20 minutes when the idea of doing four parts was discussed, and later padded out to fill the vacant space. Romero's story occasionally meanders and it takes a good half an hour for things to get weird. In the meantime, despite Barbeau's performance, we care so little about these self-centred characters that it's hard to remain interested. Argento's breathless camerawork keeps his episode more watchable and his constant nods to Poe make for a fun movie-going experience. Romero is capable of the same sort of grandeur, but on this occasion it appears as if his heart simply wasn't in it.

American Nightmare: Romero's *Valdemar* is a fable, a story with a moral about the corrupting power of money. Coming at the tail end of the 1980s, his segment explores the decade that gave us the 'me' generation and saw people aspire to wealth at the expense of anything else. Every character here is obsessed with money. Valdemar is described as a 'ruthless old man who treats people like they're possessions', and his lawyer and nurse just want to get paid. Even Robert's hypnosis device is shaped like the pyramid on the back of a dollar bill.

Robert and Jessica are typical 1980s yuppies: him in a pinstripe shirt with slicked-back hair and her power dressing with big shoulder pads and all the jewellery she can carry. She's like an extra from *Dynasty*. They exploit a dying old man to get his fortune and talk about wealth as a precursor to sex. 'Just think of it,' says a breathless Jessica as Robert puts his hand down her blouse, 'a million dollars for us to share.' In the end both come face to face with horrors unleashed by their greed and, for Romero, an all-consuming love of money can only end badly. The final shot is a close up of blood drizzling into a suitcase full of $100 bills. Whilst far from subtle, it's an indignant image typical of Romero.

From the Vault: Tom Savini makes a brief cameo in *The Black Cat* as the man who murders his cousin and removes her teeth. He insisted on doing the scene in Victorian garb. It was even in his contract.

Verdict: Of the two parts, Argento's is the superior and the director has clearly invested more of himself into making the project work. His visual flair coupled with Keitel's nutty performance has created a darkly entertaining ride through Poe's imagination. 2/5

Night of the Living Dead (1990)
There is a fate worse than death.

Crew: Director: Tom Savini, Producers: John A. Russo & Russ Streiner, Writer: George A. Romero, Cinematographer: Frank Prinzi, Editor: Tom Dubensky, Production Designer: Cletus R. Anderson, Composer: Paul McCollough, Special Make-Up Effects: John Vulich & Everett Burrell

Cast: Tony Todd (Ben), Patricia Tallman (Barbara), Tom Towles (Harry), McKee Anderson (Helen), William Butler (Tom), Kate Finneran (Judy Rose), Bill Mosley (Johnnie), Heather Mazur (Sarah)
85 mins

Ripping Yarn: The full moon rises. In a bleak American grave-yard, Johnnie and his sister Barbara lay a wreath on their mother's grave. In the distance, between the grey headstones, a man is watching. He is old and confused. Out of nowhere a strange creature attacks Barbara and kills Johnnie. Barbara narrowly escapes and runs and hides in an abandoned farm-house. Blood drips through the ceiling and this house is hiding more grotesque creatures. The dead walk.

Into the house comes Ben, a stranger out of gas and looking for refuge. With Barbara's help he rids the building of zombies and together they board up the house and wait for help. But the noise only attracts more of the walking dead and they quickly become surrounded. Unbeknownst to them there are people in the basement: middle-aged man Harry Copper, his wife, his sick child, and farm boy Tom and his girlfriend Judy Rose.

Harry demands they barricade themselves in the cellar and wait for help but Ben wants to find gas for his truck and drive the group to safety. As the men bicker, Barbara begins to regain her strength. She watches the dead things move outside the window and sees that in the open they are slow and clumsy. You could just walk right past them and, as the night grows darker, it's a theory she may have to put into practice…

Making a Monster: 'From my standpoint, this is purely financial,'[3] stated Romero on the *Night of the Living Dead* remake. A copyrighting error on the original had seen the film go instantly into the public domain, meaning the boys at Image Ten barely made a cent. Various lawsuits followed and a colourised version was released to try and regain ownership. The remake was another such attempt and Romero's comment shows it was hardly a labour of love.

Most of the original ten were back, with Russ Streiner and John Russo acting as producers. Despite agreeing to write and executive produce, Romero had no interest in returning as director and instead demanded the job be given to his friend Tom Savini. Many of the team were also directors (John Russo shot 1982's *Midnight*) and had been hoping to helm the project themselves. But above all, for marketing purposes, they needed Romero's name on the movie and so reluctantly agreed.

Though Savini had directed episodes of *Tales from the Darkside* it would be his feature-film debut and he arrived excited and brimming with ideas. In a nod to the original he wanted to start the film in black and white and slowly dissolve into colour. He also wanted to never refer to the creatures as zombies and show extreme scenes of violence to remind people of the brutality of death. All these ideas were rejected. On set, Russo and Streiner were ever present and demanded things be done their way. With Romero working on *The Dark Half*, Savini was alone and all his ideas were tossed aside. 'I knew a lot more than I was able to do on that film,'[4] he later stated.

Production began in Pittsburgh in April 1990 with a budget of $4.2 million. It was a rigid three-month shoot with 13-hour 'days' filmed mainly after dark. The cast included Tony Todd (who later found acclaim as the iconic *Candyman* in 1992) and *Knightriders*' Patricia Tallman and Tom Towles from *Henry: Portrait of a Serial Killer* (1986). With the exception of Tallman, all the actors bore a striking resemblance to their 1968 counterparts.

Savini's attempt to show a realistic violence ran into trouble when the MPAA granted the film an X. Aware that this would severely damage the box office, the producers happily cut the movie. This was, after all, a film made purely to make money. With his ideas rejected and the film's guts torn out, the final result was a far cry from what he intended. Savini was heart-broken and he remembers the experience as 'the worst night-mare'[5] of his life. *Night 1990* premiered at Hollywood's Chinese Theatre and made an initial $3 million before gradually slumping at the box office. Today it remains relatively forgotten by fans of the genre.

The Splatter Factor: In the light of a number of zombie spoofs that littered popular culture (such as Michael Jackson's *Thriller* music video and *Return of the Living Dead*) Savini wanted to make his creatures scary again by really capturing what death was like. To achieve this, special-effects men John Vulich and Everett Burrell (who were Savini's apprentices on *Day)* viewed forensic photos and visited real autopsies. As a result the walking dead here are jaundiced, with milky eyes and bodies that look as if the blood inside them has somehow gone stale. There's even an autopsied zombie with a sewn-up chest as a grim reminder of where the team got their inspiration.

The *Night* remake contained a number of groundbreaking effects techniques. Gunshot wounds, usually achieved by actors wearing squibs underneath their clothes, are here seen splitting through the bare chest of a half-naked zombie. This was achieved by building an appliance upon his real torso and hiding squibs underneath – a simple but effective way to push the boundaries of splatter. The department, however, was not without problems. Whenever Romero was onset, Vulich and Burrell would actively pursue him for the chance to do effects on *The Dark Half*. It was a job that should have gone to Savini but Romero, sadly, accepted.

Digging up the Dead: The somewhat avaricious cynicism behind *Night 1990* has led to a slightly staid cinematic experience. Romero's original contained a gut fearlessness which here is replaced with by-the-numbers filmmaking and an eye on box office returns. The gnarled horror usually associated with a George Romero/Tom Savini zombie picture is also toned down and the camera cuts away whenever things get messy. A crowbar entering Uncle Rege's head and the various bullet hits produce only a small amount of squirting red stuff and Ben's nasty execution of a twisted-in-half zombie also happens off screen.

Savini's original cut was grimmer and even had a *Dawn of the Dead*-style exploding head when Tom blasts a zombie from the back of a truck. Regardless, Savini still manages to deliver a macabre eye for detail. A corpse at the top of the stairs drips blood, leaving a growing red patch on the ceiling below. Later, a zombie woman staggers across the countryside clutching a doll like a baby. In one brief instant we are given an insight into this creature's past and the sadness of a life lost.

Perhaps due to inexperience, he is less successful at generating suspense and *Night 1990* lacks tension. In the 1968 original, when Barbra first enters the farmhouse the building is draped in lurching shadows that could be hiding anything. Here, Barbara enters a building bathed in warm light that shows us every corner and lets us see every danger well in advance. The remake is perhaps also too quick on its feet, rattling through the night without stopping to explore the surrounding darkness.

Savini's direction of actors is also found wanting. Some performances are too broad and Tom Towles is a cartoonish version of Karl Hardman's Harry, ranting manically and screaming about the 'bunch of yo-yos' upstairs. The two leads, though, are more believable. As Ben, Tony Todd brings a needed gravitas to the role and stunt woman Patricia Tallman excels as Barbara, convincingly changing from a woman gripped by hysteria to someone determined to survive. 'You told me to fight. Well I'm fighting. I'm not panicking,' she tells Ben.

Barbara's transformation into a fully realised 1990s action heroine is one of the many changes Romero has brought to his new screenplay. Indeed, where the *Night* redux excels is in its knowledge of the original and its willingness to subvert audience expectation to generate real surprises. In the opening scene in the graveyard, viewers expecting the approaching figure to be a zombie are thrown off by the fact that it is actually a confused old man. The real monster then lunges out of nowhere and smashes Johnnie's head against a gravestone. Savini keeps this up till the last minute and everything we thought we knew about *Night of the Living Dead* is gleefully turned upside down.

American Nightmare: To Romero this was a chance to finally set things right. His films since *Night* strongly called for equality between the sexes but he could never forgive himself for the feeble portrayal of women in the original *Night*. Barbra is catatonic, Helen a typical housewife and Judy a ditsy and relatively useless girlfriend. Here, Barbara is an action heroine to rival Sigourney Weaver in *Aliens* (1986). Around halfway through she swaps her prissy dress for trousers (her exposed blouse looking like Bruce Willis's *Die Hard* vest) and displays a mean aim with a shotgun. While the others bicker around her, Barbara sees a potential form of escape. 'They're so slow,' she observes. 'We could just walk right past them.' In the dead of night she does just that and, heavily armed, blasts her way to safety.

For Savini's part, socio-political filmmaking isn't his thing, though in interviews he has called his zombie virus a representation of AIDS. There are similarities. The disease is spread by physical contact, both are disabling and cause lesions and deformities in the skin and both have an unknown origin. This said, Romero's zombies have always been that way and AIDS only came to global attention in the mid 1980s. In reality it seems more like a coincidence and the absence of sexuality in zombies makes the vampire a much more relevant metaphor for the disease.

From the Vault: Composer Paul McCollough wrote the first draft of *The Crazies* back in the early 1970s. During the initial stages of production, long-time Tim Burton collaborator Danny Elfman (of *Edward Scissorhands* [1990] fame) was considered for the musical score.

Undead or Alive: Though not in the same league as Romero's zombie films Savini's remake is still a valiant effort and its twist on the original leads to moments of genuine terror. 3/5

The Dark Half (1992)
Serious writer or serial killer? George is in two minds.

Crew: Director/Writer: George A. Romero, Producer: Declan Baldwin, Novel by: Stephen King, Cinematographer: Tony Pierce-Roberts, Editor: Pasquale Buba, Production Designer: Cletus Anderson, Composer: Christopher Young

Cast: Timothy Hutton (Thad Beaumont/George Stark), Amy Madigan (Liz Beaumont), Julie Harris (Reggie DeLesseps), Robert Joy (Fred Clawson), Chelsea Field (Annie Pangborn), Royal Dano (Digger Holt), Michael Rooker (Alan Pangborn) 116 mins

Ripping Yarn: Young aspiring writer Thad Beaumont can hear sparrows. Even when there's none around. His headaches are getting worse and doctors suspect a brain tumour. During an operation they discover an unborn twin absorbed into Thad's system. It has been growing. Outside, a flock of sparrows attacks the hospital.

Twenty-three years later, Thad is now a professional novelist. He has a beautiful wife, two lovely babies (twins) and has just finished his latest book. His stories are highbrow and artistic, but never make any money. Yet George Stark's books do. Stark is a badass author of trashy fiction – and he's also a pseudonym for Thad Beaumont. While teaching English at university, Thad is approached by a sleazy opportunist called Clawson who knows about his alter ego. He tries to blackmail him but Thad goes public himself and buries his alias. The story is picked up by a dozen magazines and a local photographer has him pose in front of a mock tombstone bearing the inscription: 'George Stark: Not a very nice guy.'

Suddenly people start getting murdered: the tombstone

photographer, Clawson, Thad's agent. Thad's fingerprints are all over the scene but George Stark, it appears, has found human form and dug his way out of the earth with vengeance on his mind. Thad and his evil twin cannot coexist and winged carriers who guide souls between the land of the living and dead have come for one of them – but which one? The sparrows are flying again.

Making a Monster: Richard Bachman was dead – and Stephen King killed him. At the height of his popularity King grew concerned that people were buying his novels based on his name and not the quality of the material. As a result, the *Carrie* author created Bachman, a pseudonym that allowed him to pen novels such as *Thinner* and *The Running Man* under the radar. After a journalist discovered the truth, King laid Bachman to rest and *The Dark Half*, a novel about a writer's alter ego coming to life, was a tribute to his deceased alias.

The novel's *Jekyll and Hyde* theme immediately appealed to George Romero who adapted the 480-page book into a screenplay without King's involvement. Despite the problems with *Monkey Shines*, Romero returned to Orion Pictures and was given a $15 million budget to move into production. This was more money than it cost to fund his first eight movies combined. He was a Hollywood player now. To emphasise this, *A Room with a View* (1985) cinematographer Tony Pierce-Roberts was hired to shoot and *Hellraiser* (1987) composer Christopher Young delivered the score.

For the role of Thad Beaumont/George Stark Orion wanted a star. After considering Gary Oldman, Ed Harris and Willem Dafoe, the production eventually settled on Timothy Hutton, the *Ordinary People* (1980) Oscar winner. Ironically Ed Harris's real-life spouse Amy Madigan was cast as Thad's wife, Liz. For the wizardly Rawlie DeLesseps, Romero thought of John

Hurt, but when the actor wasn't available he changed the character's sex and cast *The Haunting*'s (1963) Julie Harris. In terms of location, Pittsburgh doubled for King's original Castle Rock setting.

Production didn't go smoothly. Behind the camera Tony Pierce-Roberts was deliberate and conventional, refusing to experiment or shoot at the breakneck pace Romero was used to. In front of camera, Timothy Hutton also caused problems and his method approach clashed with Romero's blue-collar style. Bizarrely, the actor insisted on two separate trailers – one for Thad and one for Stark, but both actor and director eventually managed to get along. Elsewhere, however, there was more trouble to come.

The debt-riddled Orion Pictures began flirting with bankruptcy. Cuts needed to be made and production equipment was recalled. 'One day the trucks came and just hauled everything away,'[6] remembers Romero. The 12th reel of the film was never completed and a number of special-effects shots were left half done. Christopher Young's score wasn't finished either and parts of the track were lifted from elsewhere in the movie and pasted over the third act. The production ended in March 1991 but due to Orion's financial problems the movie wouldn't be released until 1993. The company eventually declared bankruptcy with a debt of over $690 million.

The Dark Half earned a minimal $10 million at the US box office but studios had been impressed by Romero's ability to deliver a mainstream horror picture. He was a hot property and both MGM and 20th Century Fox wanted to make a deal. Hollywood wanted another piece of Romero. It ended up swallowing him whole.

Face of Death: *The Dark Half* is Romero at his most conventional. The eccentric and jagged rhythms of his earlier movies are gone and the film lacks the experimentation that defined 1988's *Monkey Shines*. For the most part it looks like any other professional Hollywood genre movie: all generic framing and clear visuals. Tony Pierce-Roberts is a fine DOP and along with production designer Cletus Anderson has created a film full of brown shades that invest the film with a sombre tone. *The Dark Half* was shot in autumn and there is a gentle sadness to watching the trees twist and shed their life, while the crisp leaves flutter across the cold sky.

This sky also happens to be full of sparrows. They swarm on the horizon and turn it black, bringing with them an increasing sense of foreboding. These are the carriers of souls between lands and the sound of their flicking wings means doom for either Thad or Stark. Contrasting with this melancholic feel are Stark's razorblade killings – cruel and sticky and leaving remains best left to the flies. In these sequences Romero injects some invention and borrows the gaudy red-light motif from *Creepshow* whenever Stark slices someone open. There are photographer Homer Gamache's pick-up truck brake lights and the neon red that illuminates journalist Mike Donaldson's apartment hallway when he is chopped up. It's like Thad Beaumont's alter ego is a figure from hell, taking his fiery wrath with him wherever he goes.

The Splatter Factor: Tom Savini was out, replaced by his protégés John Vulich and Everett Burrell. Their principal work was with Timothy Hutton, first turning him into the malevolent cracker George Stark and later covering his face with pus-filled blemishes as his flesh deteriorates. Aside from his costume – wing-tipped boots, tight black suit, glistening silver buckle – Romero wanted Stark to look physically different from Thad, so Vulich and Burrell set about using latex to turn Stark's face into a funhouse-mirror version of Thad's. The transformation took hours to achieve and to get Hutton into a 'real George Stark mood'[7] they littered their effects trailer with half-eaten pizza and empty beer cans. Hutton's method approach was apparently contagious.

The film required a number of visual effects which were supplied by VCE (Visual Concept Engineering). Their main priority was the birds. They created the effect of thousands of sparrows swarming on the horizon through a mixture of real cutthroat finches, animatronic/taxidermy birds (with real feathers and beaks) and blue screen. Because Thad and Stark were both to be played by Hutton, effects work was also required whenever the characters were in the same shot. To achieve this, VCE used a split screen or – for scenes where the two characters had to touch – a process that involved matting Hutton's head on to the body of a stand in. This stand in was played by none other than *Martin*'s John Amplas.

Digging up the Dead: Romero's faithfulness to the original Stephen King novel saw few of his usual thematic preoccupations emerge. This is a George Romero film that could have been directed by anyone. While he and King write fundamentally about America, they approach the topic from different angles. King's novels are about ordinary Americans; people who hate their jobs and have trouble with their cars. Romero deals with the USA from a political standpoint and explores the corruption at the country's centre. In terms of studying America, Romero writes from the head and Stephen King from the heart.

Accordingly, the socio-political core of Romero's work is absent here and instead the film examines a working everyman. Thad is an ordinary guy who has unwittingly unleashed his own inner being on to the world and this Jekyll/Hyde theme is one aspect of Romero's cinema that does survive here. Stark is Thad's diametric opposite, cold and brutal where he is warm and compassionate. But he is also part of Thad. When Clawson threatens to go public with the story of Thad being Stark, the novelist fantasises about what he'd like to do to him. He'd like to 'cut off his pecker and shove it in his rat mouth'. When Stark comes alive this is exactly what his dark half does.

Thad enjoys the fictional Stark; he likes the freedom to throw off his shackles and go nuts. Writing as Stark allows him to drink heavily and to smoke like a demon, something he gave up himself three years earlier. But the novelist is too good a person to be happy when Stark begins his murders. In the end this isn't a story about unleashing the beast within; it's about exorcising it for good. 'I don't want him around any more,' says Thad and attempts to use the sparrows to send Stark 'back to the Devil'.

Romero has perhaps made Thad too clean cut for the film's own good. In King's novel, Thad is deemed fully responsible for Stark's actions. 'You did it together; you two,' exclaims Sheriff Alan Pangborn in the book. 'Thad invited you back. He did it.' The duality within Thad is something that cannot easily be got rid of and the novel ends with the question of whether his wife Liz can come to terms with that fact. In the film there is no doubt that their marriage will hold firm.

The Dark Half is a solid, professional psychological horror. It looks pretty (if vacant), the cast is credible and Christopher Young's Danny Elfman-esque score adds a layer of under-the-skin foreboding. Sadly it has few surprises and little to interest fans of Romero. As Stark goes on his killing spree there is a feeling of going through the motions and it is not until the final act that Thad and Stark finally face off. Based on this movie, Romero shows that he could have easily become a fine and anonymous mainstream filmmaker. Thankfully, that wasn't to be.

From the Vault: In 1990 Jonathan Demme went to Pittsburgh to shoot a psychological horror picture of his own – *The Silence of the Lambs*. Paying homage to the city's favourite film-maker, Demme cast Romero in a cameo as an FBI agent.

Undead or Alive: A likeable and easy-to-watch movie, but the combined efforts of Stephen King and George Romero should have produced more. There have been better King adaptations. *Misery*, released the year before *The Dark Half* was completed, is one of them. 2/5

Back from the Dead

In the early 1990s Romero was being taken seriously by the majors and together with his new partner Peter Grunwald signed a contract to work at New Line Cinema. Things were looking up. He was being paid more money than ever before and got the go ahead on a new psychological thriller called *Before I Wake* (see section entitled 'No More Room in Hell'). Two years later the movie still hadn't materialised and New Line were unhappy about the script. Then the contract ran out and Romero/Grunwald took the project to MGM. Here it went as far as set design and casting before they too backed out.

Nothing Romero could come up with was panning out. He wanted to remake *The Mummy* but that fell through. A fourth film in the *Dead* saga called *Twilight of the Dead* was planned but that never happened. Projects at major studios became cast dependent and Romero was getting questioned and second-guessed at every turn. He became frustrated by studio heads half his age. They wanted a 'yes man' – a Michael Bay or a Brett Ratner – the kind of filmmaker who has nothing to say (except what the studios tell them) and says it in the loudest way possible. Above all else, Romero had a sense of rectitude – and it kept him out of the movies for nearly a decade.

GEORGE A. ROMERO

Bruiser (2000)
Meet the new face of terror.

Crew: Director/Writer: George A. Romero, Producers: Peter Grunwald & Ben Barenholtz, Cinematographer: Adam Swica, Editor: Miume Jan Eramo, Production Designer: Sandra Kybartas, Composer: Donald Rubinstein, Special Make-Up Effects: Caligari Inc.

Cast: Jason Flemyng (Henry Creedlow), Peter Stormare (Miles), Leslie Hope (Rosemary), Nina Garbiras (Janine Creedlow), Andrew Tarbet (James). Tom Atkins (Detective McCleary)
99 mins

Ripping Yarn: Henry Creedlow is nobody, just another aspirational schmuck sleepwalking through life. He wants the good things in life: new house, fast car, hot wife, the next promotion, and he'll sacrifice anything to get them. That includes his personality and self-respect. Hell, they went years ago. Miles, his boss at *Bruiser* fashion magazine, happily belittles him in front of co-workers and Henry only smiles. 'You let people walk all over you,' bemoans his wife Janine. Henry nods. 'If that's what it takes,' he says.

With money tight and his new house only half finished, Henry plays the stock market through best friend Jimbo. The returns are never as much as he expects. At a staff barbeque, while Miles's wife Rosie makes a mask from Henry's face, across the pool Janine is giving Miles a hand job. Henry sees – and does nothing. On the drive home Janine mocks him for being so weak and she spends the night with Miles. Henry fantasises about blowing his own brains out.

When he wakes the next morning his face has vanished. No features, no eyes, no identity, just a white porcelain mask.

Henry realises that, with his new anonymity, he can do anything, go anywhere or kill anyone and get away with it. He has been ignored and overlooked for too long and the people who've hurt him are going to pay. Henry Creedlow is nobody, and he's looking for revenge...

Making a Monster: 'I'm like my zombies,' said George Romero. 'I won't stay dead.'[1] The time spent in development hell had in the most painful way possible taught Romero something he already knew – Hollywood was no place for a guy like him. For all his faults, Romero has a deep sense of integrity, perhaps the one thing studio executives find hardest to deal with, and after years of frustration he was back on the outside. In the mid-1990s Romero was approached to remake 1959's French horror *Les Yeux Sans Visage* (*Eyes Without a Face*), the story of a mutilated young woman who conceals her deformity beneath a featureless white mask. Plans for a remake collapsed, but the image of the faceless individual stayed with Romero and *Bruiser* was born (the title comes from a slang word used by Romero's daughter Tina meaning 'cool').

With a script in hand, Romero and Grunwald began to pitch it around Hollywood. To emphasise Henry's status as a nobody, Romero wanted to cast an unknown. The studios wanted Johnny Depp. At the Cannes Film Festival the script was picked up by French company Studio Canal+ who agreed to put up the $10 million budget. Romero was back, but soon found himself in unfamiliar surroundings. Shooting in America had become expensive and *Bruiser*'s low budget meant doing a feature outside of Pittsburgh for the first time.

In many ways it was a completely fresh start, but it also marked the end of something special. In films like *Martin*, Pittsburgh had become as much of a character as the actors on screen and Romero was saying goodbye to it for a final time. All he could do was pack a bag and head north. Filming would take place in Toronto, Canada on real locations. On the plus side, less money meant a more intimate team and Romero was surprised by the dedication of his Canadian crew. Even the set dresser had read the script and wanted to contribute.

The cast was equally enthusiastic. *Lock, Stock and Two Smoking Barrels'* (1998) Jason Flemyng took the lead despite having to wear a prosthetic mask for 16 hours a day. In supporting roles, Leslie Hope (later of TV's *24*) appeared as Miles's wife and *Jurassic Park: The Lost World* (1997) actor Peter Stormare was ideally cast as sex-crazed megalomaniac Miles. 'He's out to lunch,' remembered Flemyng. 'He's mad as a brush! He's like a beast let out of a metal cage.'[2]

Romero had a blast and it felt like old times: making movies out of love and surrounded by people who cared. Some old friends were there too. Pittsburgh actor Tom Atkins brought along his usual likeable dignity, and the film's jazzy score was provided by *Knightriders* composer Donald 'Dr D' Rubinstein. On the downside, finding distribution became the same old story. The majors didn't want it and, with no drive-ins or indie theatres, *Bruiser* ended up bypassing the cinema completely and going straight to DVD. Romero's big comeback was hardly seen by anybody. In the UK, at time of writing, it has not been released at all.

Face of Death: Romero's favourite film was always Michael Powell's filmed opera *Tales of Hoffmann*. In the late 1980s he planned to stage his own version, set in space, at the Pittsburgh Playhouse but the project never materialised. His love of opera never died, however, and, stylistically, *Bruiser* is the closest he's ever come to the medium. With cinematographer Adam Swica, Romero's camera sweeps through Toronto and grace-fully dances around the protagonists. When Henry begins to exact his brutal vengeance, he catches his wife half naked in Miles's boardroom. As he stalks her around the room, she takes refuge under the table and, in one shot, the camera glides up across the room and then down under the table with her. The film almost outshines *Monkey Shines* in the whirly camera stakes.

At the film's conclusion, Miles throws a masked ball with a grotesque horror theme. People arrive dressed as devils, witches and freaks. Henry shows up in a long black cloak and wide black hat like the Phantom of the Opera. Hiding amongst the shadows, Henry is a creature of the night. Then there's his white pantomime face: cold, featureless and uncaring. Henry's own blankness dominates the surroundings and the film's key aesthetic is of icy whites occasionally smeared with blood. There are walls the colour of office paper, Henry's sterile, unfinished home and the chalk-coloured club house. Even Tom Atkins's hair is white. Henry's world may be operatic, but it is also a blank canvas waiting to be painted on.

Digging up the Dead: Seven years is a long time. But the man who wandered out of the filmmaking wilderness had somehow found himself in the process. *Bruiser* is the work of the Romero of old – the socially conscious director of *Martin* and *The Crazies* – and the film is all the stronger for it. It is not a subtle film, but is instead a wild twenty-first-century parable: the faceless office drone who loses his personality completely to climb the corporate ladder.

Henry Creedlow believes in America, believes in how it works. You work hard, do as you're told, get a credit card, marry and reproduce. He can't stand up for himself or show individuality unless it threatens his tenuous social standing. In his life, 'bosses are entitled' – even if it means letting them sleep with your wife. Henry wants to be like his buddy Jimbo, a man who has built a personality out of possessions. 'If I could fuck a car,' says Jimbo, 'I would never leave my garage.'

Losing his face is not just an expression of what he's let himself become; it also represents a blank slate – the chance to build a new personality from scratch. This being a Romero film, Henry builds it in blood and butchers those who've wronged him. After each murder, Henry's white face becomes tainted. First it is sprayed by his housekeeper's wet, red wound, and then, after killing Janine, he paints sticky blood over his eyes and cheeks. It's like he's applying war paint.

The theme of being a faceless member of society is hammered home: 'I'm invisible. I've always been invisible,' cries Henry, long after we've got the point. But Romero never forgets to keep things entertaining. Henry is likeable and his boss, best friend and wife are vile enough to keep us on his side. As a writer Romero delivers his usual brand on quotable one-liners. 'You're telling me you've never stuck your dick up another man's sandwich?' Miles asks a bemused Tom Atkins. He is both lyrical and obscene at the same time.

The film strays into the supernatural with the sudden appearance of the white face, but, given that the film is essentially a morality tale, it hardly seems to matter. Indeed, *Bruiser* could be read as a dream, with the events taking place in Henry's head. This would be in keeping with his frustrated fantasies at the start of the film where he shoots himself and axes his wife to death. If anything, *Bruiser* is a beautifully crafted companion piece to *Martin*. Both deal with male outsiders driven to dysfunction by society and Henry shares Martin's sweet vulnerability and brimming violence.

Henry is a killer for the modern age, one who is tired of being shoved around by people with power. After his enforced hiatus, Romero no doubt felt the same way about Hollywood producers. *Bruiser* is his own frustrated daydream.

American Nightmare: On 20 April 1999 the Columbine massacre horrified America. Two students shot dead a teacher and 12 fellow pupils, injuring 24 more. They ended by killing themselves. For them, school was a living hell and they were bullied daily. The teachers did their best to ignore it. On his website one of the boys wrote, 'Whatever I do people make fun of me, and sometimes directly to my face. I'll get my revenge soon enough.' For George Romero it was simple: 'That event pointed to the fact that society could create monsters.'[3] *Bruiser* is not directly about Columbine, but the ghost of that day drifts through the film.

Henry is a man who has no voice; a man degraded by the world around him. He is seen as worthless, easy to step over, and has an innocence about him that allows him to 'eat whatever shit is served up', as his wife tells him. He's desperate to please: organising parties for his boss and trying to build his wife a dream home. He's like a kid. But in the end the torment gets too much for him and, like a kid, he finds his emotions hard to control. The film does not condone Henry's actions, but at least allows us to look at things from his point of view – and from the point of view of America's real-life monsters.

From the Vault: The scene of the fancy dress party at the film's conclusion features cameos from Romero's then wife Christine and their two children, Tina and Andrew. Christine is dressed as *The Bird with the Crystal Plumage*, a reference to Dario Argento's 1969 slasher of the same name.

Undead or Alive: A wonderful return from a master of the genre. It was a relief to have him back. 'Bruiser. Fucking bruiser, man.' 4/5

Land of the Dead (2005)
The dead shall inherit the earth.

Crew: Director/Writer: George A. Romero, Producers: Mark Canton, Bernie Goldmann & Peter Grunwald, Cinematographer: Miroslaw Baszak, Editor: Michael Doherty, Production Designer: Arv Greywal, Composers: Reinhold Heil & Johnny Klimek, Special Make-Up Effects: Greg Nicotero & Howard Berger

Cast: Simon Baker (Riley), Dennis Hopper (Kaufman), Asia Argento (Slack), Robert Joy (Charlie), Eugene Clark (Big Daddy), John Leguizamo (Cholo)
97 mins

Working Titles: *Twilight of the Dead, Dead Reckoning*

Ripping Yarn: Fiddler's Green is a towering sky rise surrounded by water. Kaufman and his army have transformed it into a fort and live in the luxurious penthouses with those who can afford it. Everyone else huddles together in the slums at ground zero. The rest of America belongs to the dead.

Riley is a scavenger, the leader of a small crew raiding supplies for Kaufman. His friend Charlie, a crack marksman severely burnt in a fire, keeps an eye on him. They hunt by night in a massively armoured vehicle called Dead Reckoning and obliterate any zombie that gets within 100 yards. On the street, Big Daddy is watching. He's a dead gas-station attendant who is regaining primary functions. Seeing zombies being wiped out, he leads a small group of the dead towards the city – bent on revenge.

Cholo, Riley's second in command, has made enough money for a penthouse apartment, but his lower-class background makes him an undesirable. Angered, he steals Dead Reckoning and aims the vehicle's missiles at the tower. Kaufman has until midnight to give him $5 million or he'll reduce the Green to ashes. Instead, the big man sends Riley, Charlie and former prostitute Slack to get his vehicle back. But Riley has plans of his own. Meanwhile the dead have reached the river separating them from Fiddler's Green. Big Daddy hangs a foot over the side and drops down into the black water. On the surface of the riverbed below, he begins to walk…

Making a Monster: 'Resident Evil may well be shit, but if it wasn't for that movie's success I wouldn't have got to make Land of the Dead,'[4] stated Romero. The early part of the twenty-first century was beginning to feel like it belonged to the dead. Romero had considered doing a third Night sequel for years and in 2001 finally delivered a screenplay based on his aborted Day script. But following the tragic events of 9/11, studio heads began to worry about the scripted scenes of global terror and the film was shelved.

Then came the pandemic. Zombie feature Resident Evil (2002) cleaned up at the box office. So did 28 Days Later the same year. And 2004's Dawn of the Dead remake. Hollywood executives could sniff profit amongst the rotting corpses and it was only a matter of time before the father of the living dead got a reprieve. Atmosphere Entertainment picked up the film and along with Universal Studios (who were also behind the Dawn remake) supplied a $15 million budget. Romero was working with few of his previous collaborators, but one link to his past came in the form of Dario Argento's daughter, Asia.

He had known her since she was a kid and Asia had grown up to become a strong movie actress (appearing in her father's Trauma [1993] and later xXx [2002] with Vin Diesel). Though she had vowed never to appear in a horror movie not directed by Dario, she made an exception for George. He was virtually family anyway. Shooting took place in 2004 in the Toronto winter with an all-star cast, a fact that disturbed many fans. Yet it seems unlikely that the film would have been made without them and cast members included *Moulin Rouge*'s (2001) John Leguizamo and *Easy Rider* star Dennis Hopper. On set, Romero, still an ardent political radical, was stunned to see a different man to the counterculture icon he expected: 'Who knew he was a republican? Goddamn it! *Easy Rider* wears plaid golf pants,'[5] exclaimed Romero.

Land of the Dead was released in summer 2005 and Universal was confident of a hit. So much so that Romero rewrote the ending to allow for a sequel with the same characters – a first for the series. But on the big screen the film struggled and Universal cancelled sequel plans. It fared better on DVD and the small-screen version seemed closer to what Romero intended. For cinemas, he had been contracted to release the picture as an R, but on DVD *Land* got an X certificate in the vein of *Dawn* and *Day*. At present the film stands as the last in the continuing saga. For his next project Romero stayed with zombies but approached it from a different angle. He went back to that very first night.

Face of Death: *Land of the Dead* is a film that lives by night. The nightmarish landscape seems permanently bathed in blue moonlight – from the opening shot in the churchyard, where dead musicians on a bandstand eerily blow into their brass instruments, to the shuffling zombies emerging from the inky river to lay waste to Fiddler's Green. Mankind, it seems, has finally entered the darkness for good. Even in the few scenes that take place in the day there is no sun. As Riley and Charlie wander through the deserted Pittsburgh streets, their world is just grey concrete, brown walls and black clouds. The wind whips through the buildings and what light there is just illustrates how alone they are.

But this darkness is also a hiding place (a recurring theme for Romero) and any attempts to break it usually results in cataclysm. Fiddler's Green is the only building with power for miles around, but its burning yellow lights act as a beacon to Big Daddy and his army of the undead. A torchlight sequence where Riley and a solider look for ammo reveals in the beam Bosch-like horrors straight from hell. Towards the conclusion the attack of the dead results in an explosion that climbs up into the funereal black sky. The Halloween-orange fire can be seen for miles and is a sign that death is coming for the survivors at the Green.

The Splatter Factor: Since apprenticing under Tom Savini on *Day of the Dead*, Greg Nicotero and Howard Burger had gone on to form KNB (with Robert Kurtzman), one of the most successful special-effects studios in Hollywood. Their work on *From Dusk till Dawn* (1996), *Kill Bill* (2003), etc. kept them in constant demand, but working with Romero was special. Nicotero was a Pittsburgh kid and George was his hero. Rather than build the usual furrowed, caveman-ish brow for the zombies (as with *Day*), they went about creating something new. In *Land*, the undead walk around with rotting, pus-covered faces. They are starved and some are virtual skeletons. Their mouths are rotten too, dead and black, and their eyes are full of exploded blood vessels.

In the R-rated version the gore is less pronounced. Rather than cut it, Romero inserted CGI zombies to walk in front of the camera to obscure anything grisly. The film used a number of computer effects (over 300), the most obvious being a priest whose head hangs off and is connected to his body only by a few fleshy tendons. Elsewhere Nicotero and his team have created some truly memorable 'gags'. A cheek is torn off, a face kicked off, a person is grabbed by his upper lip and his whole face peeled back over his skull leaving a screaming red mess. The standout, though, is a zombie with her arm stuck shoulder deep down someone's throat – reaching in for the sloppy insides. Savini would be proud.

Digging up the Dead: Forgetting the claustrophobic nihilism of its predecessors, *Land of the Dead* takes us out on to the streets of a post-apocalyptic Pittsburgh for some down-and-dirty action. Characters leap on to moving vehicles, things explode, Cholo fires a harpoon gun, there are gun battles (even the zombies tool up) and a gladiatorial fight when former prostitute Slack is tossed in an arena with the salivating dead. This isn't a horror movie – it's *Mad Max* with zombies.

Riley is a noble, square-jawed, blonde-haired hero – the type of guy who gives medicine to sick kids. He's like John Wayne. Indeed, *Land* borrows key motifs from the western, with Kaufman acting as the corrupt cattle baron hiring Riley's sheriff to track down the outlaw Cholo. Riley's team are professionals in the Howard Hawks/*Rio Bravo* (1959) mode. Riley designed and built Dead Reckoning; his friend Charlie is an expert marksman. (When a soldier offers him a machinegun, Charlie turns it down. 'This piece fires 14 rounds per second,' argues the soldier. 'I don't normally need that many,' is Charlie's honest reply.)

The action in *Land* is less tongue-in-cheek than *Dawn*, but still has its fair share of dark humour and wicked one-liners. There's the bar where you can 'take your picture with a zombie' (featuring a cameo from *Shaun of the Dead*'s Edgar Wright and Simon Pegg) and the now iconic line, 'Zombies, man. They freak me out,' delivered by a nose-picking Dennis

Hopper. This said, beneath the jokes and high-octane set pieces, there is an acute sadness. After all, this is a world plagued by death; a world where, as Riley states, 'everyone has a story' consisting of loss and pain and despair.

Perhaps the saddest of all is zombie revolutionary Big Daddy. As the raiders tear apart his town, he witnesses his own kind being mindlessly obliterated. When a zombie standing next to him loses its head, Daddy's resulting death moan is both chilling and tragic. The *Dead* films are famous for casting black actors as heroes (Duane Jones in *Night*, Ken Foree in *Dawn* and Terry Alexander in *Day*) and Eugene Clark's Big Daddy fits the bill more easily than blue-eyed-boy Baker. This time out, Romero's sympathies are totally with his living dead.

Perhaps because of its uninhibited spectacle or perhaps because a generation of us have grown up watching the *Dead* films on home video, *Land* seems to work better on the small screen. The splatter added to the X-certificate version ('18' in the UK) is in keeping with its predecessors (a high point being a soldier having his arm chopped off and then falling on an exploding grenade). But the film also feels more intimate and grungier. The Hollywood budget, slick cinematography and movie-star casting have dulled the film's bite, but on DVD they all seem less overstated. For Romero smaller has always been better.

American Nightmare: Romero always planned to direct a zombie picture once a decade, with each movie reflecting the mood and socio-political climate of that era. He missed out in the 1990s but in the early twenty-first century there was only one issue on America's mind – 9/11. *Land* takes on the Bush Administration directly. Kaufman is George W. (though Dennis Hopper is said to have based him on Donald Rumsfeld), a man running a country based on the politics of fear. He offers people safety within the Green but at the price of their freedom. Anyone not toeing the line is locked away without trial or sent into the zombie arena (an undead Guantanamo Bay). Kaufman looks after the wealthy ('the haves and the have mores'[6] as Bush would refer to them) and leaves the poor to freeze on the streets below.

When Cholo steals Dead Reckoning and demands a $5 million ransom, Kaufman refuses on the grounds that, 'We don't negotiate with terrorists.' Cholo then comments, 'Kaufman's gonna pay, man, or he knows I'm gonna do a jihad on his ass.' The war in Iraq is also referred to, with the huge demonstration of firepower by Dead Reckoning – recklessly gunning down zombies in suburban areas – identical to the actions of American tanks in Baghdad. 'I thought this was gonna be a battle,' says a new recruit. 'It's a fucking massacre.' George Romero, as always, is political but rarely subtle.

From the Vault: In 2005, *Land of the Dead*'s main rival at the box office was Steven Spielberg's *War of the Worlds*, a project Romero himself had been attached to in the early 1990s.

Undead or Alive: Perhaps not as vital as its three prequels but still an entertaining and action-packed ride into zombiedom. Nobody does the undead quite like Romero. 3/5

Diary of the Dead (2007)
Shoot the dead.

Crew: Director/Writer: George A. Romero, Producers: Peter Grunwald, Artur Spigel, Sam Englebardt, Ara Katz, Cinematographer: Adam Swica, Editor: Michael Doherty, Production Designer: Rupert Lazarus, Composer: Norman

Orenstein, Special Make-Up Effects: Gaslight Studio supervised by Greg Nicotero

Cast: Michelle Morgan (Debra), Josh Close (Jason Creed), Shawn Roberts (Tony), Amy Lalonde (Tracy), Joe Dinicol (Eliot), Scott Wentworth (Maxwell), Philip Riccio (Ridley), Chris Violette (Gordo), Tatiana Maslany (Mary)
95 mins

Ripping Yarn: October 24th. Seven student filmmakers shoot a 'mummy movie' in a Pittsburgh forest. The director, Jason Creed, would prefer to be making documentaries and when the radio announces that the dead are returning to life he finally sees his chance. With a camera in hand, Jason plans to film the real events as they unfold and the world quickly falls apart. His film will be called *The Death of Death*.

Ridley (the mummy himself) heads to his parents' mansion, which he describes as a virtual fortress. The rest of the group, including the hard-drinking Professor Maxwell, jump in a Winnebago and leave town. Jason's girlfriend Deb wants to be with her family and the students drive her home. Along the way they are attacked by a dead cop — 'He wants more than your licence and registration!' — and Mary, a staunch Catholic, runs over several zombies in their escape. Traumatised, she pulls over and shoots herself in the face. Jason continues to film.

Mary is not dead and they take her to a nearby hospital. It has long since been abandoned — at least by anything living. The news continues to show the dead rising across the world and people everywhere are broadcasting their own personal take on Armageddon. Jason sees the catastrophe as a gift from God, a chance to make a name for himself as a documentary filmmaker. The question is: who's going to be left to watch?

Making a Monster: Though *Land of the Dead* had met with a mixed response from the Romero faithful, there was at least a sense of relief that accompanied the movie. After his time in the wilderness and the non-release of *Bruiser*, Romero was now back in our cinemas. He had completed his *Dead* saga and fans were looking forward to something new; maybe one of his lost projects like *Diamond Dead* or *From a Buick 8* (see the 'No More Room in Hell' section). What he did next surprised everyone. He went back to the beginning.

Romero was getting old. He had moved permanently to Canada, split from his wife of 26 years and the last thing he wanted was to waste time developing ideas with Hollywood execs. For his next film he decided to return to his gonzo roots and to try and recapture his independent freedom. Typically, he was going to do it with zombies. In 1989, *Book of the Dead*, a collection of short stories by famous horror writers (including Stephen King), delved into Romero's universe and speculated on what was happening around the world on that first night – when the dead began to walk. Romero liked the concept and thought to himself, 'Well, I could do that.'[7]

His first thought was to turn it into a television series and he began to develop the idea with Peter Grunwald and *Day of the Dead* composer John Harrison. When that didn't materialise he transformed it into a movie script that followed a bunch of film students making a movie when 'the shit hits the fan'.[8] The movie was not to be an official entry into his *Dead* saga. 'This is ground zero,'[9] stated Romero – a franchise reboot. His fans were mortified. To them the saga was over and anything else felt like a cheap knockoff. This was the work of an old man trying to squeeze one last dollar out of (excuse the pun) a dead franchise.

Diary went into production in Toronto at the end of 2006 and Romero spent a meagre 20 days working in the icy

Canadian weather. The film was to be a 'mockumentary', a quasi-*Blair Witch Project* (1998) with the zombie action recorded firsthand. As a result, Romero and *Bruiser* DOP Adam Swica shot using digital cameras and the budget came in at under $5 million. To emphasise the reality, Romero cast relative unknowns, including Josh Close from *The Exorcism of Emily Rose* (2005), Amy Lalonde from Canada's *Scream TV* and Shawn Roberts who had worked with Romero on *Land*.

In 2007 the film was picked up for distribution by Harvey Weinstein's Miramax, and on the festival circuit (which included a return to Sundance for the first time since *Martin*) *Diary* generated good reviews. So much so that a direct sequel is currently in the works. *Diary 2* will follow the survivors of part one to a desert island overrun by walking cadavers. Romero fans are already turning in their graves.

Face of Death: Outside a low-rent housing complex a news team report the story of a father who murdered his family and then turned the gun on himself. The reporter gives a calm analysis while in the background the bodies are carried away – until their eyes open and they start walking. *Diary of the Dead* is made up entirely of news footage, online blogs and amateur video recordings of the dead rising. The bulk comes from *The Death of Death*, a documentary by Jason Creed. His girlfriend Deb edits and provides the voiceover and *Diary* is shot vérité style. The camera slips out of focus, the battery runs low and the dead stumble about in the distance. This adds a reality to the attacks and places the viewer firmly into the situation with the filmmakers.

It is admirable that, this late in his career, Romero is trying something new, yet *Diary* seems afraid to let go of its theatrical leanings. Early on, Deb, in voiceover, explains that she has added eerie music and edited the footage to scare viewers.

Ridley's mansion is littered with security cameras and Romero uses these to be more cinematic, switching CCTV perspectives and getting different angles as the group wander down dark corridors; like an ordinary horror movie would. It's as if he's saying reality isn't enough – a comment on the nature of twenty-first-century news or a filmmaker who has failed to create a scary picture without cinema's usual bag of tricks?

The Splatter Factor: The docu-style of *Diary* has resulted in the most tepid splatter action of any of the *Dead* movies. Whereas *Dawn* and *Day* revelled in close-up sequences of twisted zombie carnage, *Diary* is forced to take a back seat and events are recorded from a distance or on shaky handheld cameras. Production photos testify that the extreme nature was there (such as a burnt cop with a hideous, weeping face) but these ravaged ghouls are hardly glimpsed in the final cut. The film does, however, have moments. There's a zombie whose brains are fried using a hospital defibrillator (resulting in her eyes boiling out of their sockets) and another whose head slowly melts after being doused in acid.

Effects were overseen by *Land of the Dead*'s Greg Nicotero but the bulk of the bloody stuff was handled by Gaslight Studios. The group comprised three disparate make-up men who individually had worked on *Saw III* (2006), *The Descent* (2005) and *Jason X* (2001). This being set on the very first night, the team decided to keep their work subtle, mainly giving the undead discoloured eyes, pallid faces and vicious, protruding teeth. Despite ranting in pre-production that he regretted the use of CGI on *Land*, Romero again overuses it. To keep the production moving, bullet hits were done on computer, a factor that displaces the film's intended naturalism. It's at this point that you start to miss Tom Savini.

Digging up the Dead: There is no getting away from the fact that this is one of Romero's weakest films, and the main reason comes down to the director's mishandling of the first-person premise. Since the newsreel vérité of *Night*, Romero's style has become almost comic book, highlighting his films as broad satires. Here that style is out of place and undermines the reality. Weird, cartoonish characters bob in and out of the narrative: like a wisecracking looter and a deaf-mute Amish fellow who refuses to bear arms but instead tosses sticks of dynamite. They're like rejects from *Creepshow*.

The dialogue, too, is laughable when sprouted by 'real' characters. 'It used to be us against us,' says heroine Debra. 'Now it's us against them... except they are us.' In *Blair Witch* the actors were encouraged to improvise to add authenticity, but here Romero's heavy-handed scripting makes his stars look incompetent. As Professor Maxwell, Scott Wentworth gets the worst of it with some absurd, Rambo-esque lines – his 'In wartime, killing comes easy' is a particular low point. Romero doesn't care and his characters are only there to voice a political sermon. The film uses the first-person perspective to attack the MySpace/YouTube generation – a generation of people who, when faced with disasters like 9/11 and Hurricane Katrina, 'don't stop to help, [they] stop to look,' as Deb observes. Sadly, this theme has taken over completely from character.

Jason is far from likeable, recording candidly when his girlfriend breaks down crying or refusing to help when Tracy is mauled by a zombie. The idea that anyone could film in the midst of such atrocities is farfetched, but Romero gets away with it by convincing us Jason is obsessed and will do anything to make a name for himself as a docu-filmmaker. 'It's a part of history,' he says. Where the premise falls down is when other characters take over shooting. Deb has been aghast at Jason's coldness – 'If it didn't happen on camera, it's like it didn't really happen, right?' she says sarcastically – but happily takes over the camerawork when asked to do so. This isn't done from character motivation; it's done because, if no one were filming, the entire premise would fall apart. As a result, *Diary* feels contrived.

The worst thing about *Diary* is its self-referential, *Scream*-like tone. Girls in scary movies always show their breasts, Romero tells us – perhaps not at his most insightful. The film is packed with similar instances. We have jokes about running zombies, references to Pittsburgh and, worst of all when Jason is making a horror movie, his lecturer applauds his film for containing 'an underlined thread of social satire'. This is Romero at his most self-satisfied.

On its 2008 release, *Diary* went toe-to-toe with *Cloverfield*, a monster movie also told from a subjective viewpoint. It doesn't help Romero that everything he gets wrong, that film gets right. The difference is simply that *Cloverfield* focuses on character rather than overbearing social commentary. It also had the confidence to play it straight and Romero, for once, could learn a thing or two.

American Nightmare: 'When there were three [news] networks,' Romero has stated, 'there were three lies. Now there are 400,000 bloggers and 400,000 lies.'[10] In *Diary*, Romero turns his attention to the sharing of information online and expresses a concern that, without media regulations, people can say whatever they like and pass it off as fact. Jason and Debra manipulate the truth around them. When his friends walk into a building, Jason asks them to do it again – so he can record it for dramatic effect. For her part, Debra edits the film with spooky music and cuts footage to make it frightening. She claims she is 'planning to scare you so you'll wake up', but this is basically another form of misinformation.

The speed with which information is shared is another cause for concern and when Jason downloads his edited footage online he gets 72,000 hits in eight minutes. Romero views this as dangerous. In interviews he has claimed that, by spreading this manipulated truth so quickly, a person like Hitler could gain power and support. He has missed the point. The problem with the Internet isn't that people will follow a good 'blogger' like sheep; it's that they're too busy writing their own blogs to care. There are maybe 400,000 lies on the Internet but there are also 400,000 people not listening. Interestingly, lack of communication used to be a major theme in Romero's work.

From the Vault: Jason's documentary *The Death of Death* was also the title of a comic book Romero wrote in 2004 under DC's *Toe Tags* series. The comic featured talking zombies, undead armies and pet elephants. It was more fun than this.

Undead or Alive: *Diary of the Dead* seems like a sad note to end on. Romero is a skilled filmmaker and there are surely great films still in him. Sadly, this isn't one of them. Perhaps it's simply about time he laid the dead to rest – permanently.
1/5

Children of the Living Dead

If imitation is the most sincere form of flattery then, by now, George Romero must be tired of the constant adulation. Since the release of *Night of the Living Dead* in 1968 his films have been copied, paid homage to, parodied and just plain ripped off. The 'borrowing' began in earnest with 1972's *Children Shouldn't Play with Dead Things*, a zombie comedy that was part *Night*, part *Scooby Doo*. *Dawn of the Dead* pushed Romero's zombies even deeper into our popular culture and his undead creatures began popping up in everything from Italian horror movies like *Zombie Creeping Flesh* (1980) to Michael Jackson music videos. It didn't end there.

Today there are low-budget genre movies like 2005's *Day of the Dead 2: Contagium* (no relation to Romero's *Day*); there are videogames like *Resident Evil* and *Dead Rising*; books such as *The Zombie Survival Guide* (2004) by Max Brooks; and comics like *The Walking Dead* and *Marvel Zombies*, which see famous superheroes like Captain America and Wolverine gripped by zombification. There was a loud and vacuous *Dawn of the Dead* remake in 2004, and in the future there are plans for a zombie TV series in the vein of *Heroes* (2007) and also remakes of *Day of the Dead* and *The Crazies*. The dead are everywhere and over the next few pages we examine some of their most interesting, Romero-inspired incarnations.

Zombi 2 (1979)
We are going to eat you.

Crew: Director: Lucio Fulci, Producers: Ugo Tucci & Fabrizio De Angelis, Writer: Elisa Briganti, Special Effects & Make-Up Supervisor: Giannetto De Rossi

Cast: Tisa Farrow (Anne), Ian McCulloch (Peter), Richard Johnson (Dr Menard)
91 mins

Alternative Title: *Zombie Flesh Eaters*

Ripping Yarn: A deserted sailboat drifts into Staten Island in New York. Two harbour cops board and, below deck, find the cabin thick with rotten food and crawling insects. From a cupboard, a fat creature lunges and kills one of them. Reporter Peter West is assigned to investigate and comes across Anne, whose father owns the abandoned sailboat. He is missing and together they try to find out what happened. Their search takes them to a Caribbean island where Dr Menard is studying a voodoo phenomenon that causes dead people to walk. This freak occurrence is happening regularly and, when Anne and Peter arrive, the island is overrun by festering zombies. Back in New York, the dead cop lies still on the autopsy slab. But for how long?

Digging up the Dead: *Zombi* (aka *Dawn of the Dead*) was a massive hit in Italy and, on the back of Dario Argento's involvement, was a subject of keen interest for genre fans thirsty for blood. The resulting splatter did not disappoint and, to capitalise on its success, *Zombi 2* was rushed into production – minus the involvement of Argento and Romero. Director Lucio

Fulci (who previously made the Italian western *Four of the Apocalypse* in 1975) made no bones about 'ripping off' their masterpiece. 'After all,' he observed, 'zombies belong to Haiti and Cuba, not to Dario Argento.'[1]

Indeed, the movie bears little resemblance to *Dawn* and, though it borrows the film's extreme gore, it is more in tune with earlier voodoo-inspired pictures such as Val Lewton's *I Walked with a Zombie* (1943). The Caribbean location emphasises this and Fulci happily sinks into the occult roots of the walking dead. Dr Menard is desperate to find a scientific explanation for the zombie uprising, but consistently comes back to voodoo black magic. His assistant Lucas lives in fear of 'the Devil' and tribal drums pound consistently from deep within the forest. 'It never pays to ignore native superstition,' tourist Brian later observes.

Fulci's piece of 'spaghetti horror' is devoid of the social commentary vital to Romero's classic and this is exploitation in its purest terms. The director also appears less interested in people and the two-dimensional characters lack depth. In the lead roles, Tisa Farrow (sister of Mia) and Ian McCulloch go through the motions; investigating, getting chased and falling in love just as you'd expect. Brian and Susan, the American couple who sail them to the island, are even blander, just two good-looking people ready to take their tops off and get eaten by zombies as the script demands. It isn't easy to care about any of the characters.

But then so what? That was never Fulci's intention and the film instead focuses on horror set pieces and scenes of savagery. *Zombi 2* is a tour de force and even manages to outdo *Dawn* in the gore stakes. The film sees zombies tied head-to-foot in white sheets and when shot in the head their pink insides flick through the offending bullet hole. Then there's the legendary sequence where a zombie hand crashes through a wooden door, grabs a woman by her hair and pulls her eyeball towards a sharp, dagger-like splinter. Like Romero, Fulci doesn't cut away.

Special Effects expert Giannetto De Rossi used his experience (he worked on 1974s *The Living Dead at the Manchester Morgue*) to eclipse Tom Savini's blue/grey monsters. Here the walking corpses are more believably disgusting; with dry crusted skin and dried green vomit around their mouths. Fulci revels in the bug-infested grossness and with films like *City of the Living Dead* (1980) and *The Beyond* (1981) cemented his reputation as Italy's premier zombie maestro.

Undead or Alive: The film is less serious and detailed than Romero's masterpiece but it is no less fun. After all, how could you refuse a movie that offers an underwater zombie doing battle with a shark? 4/5

Return of the Living Dead (1984)
They're back from the grave and ready to party!

Crew: Director/Writer: Dan O'Bannon, Producer: Tom Fox, Special Make-Up Effects: Bill Munns

Cast: Clu Gulager (Burt), James Karen (Frank), Linnea Quigley (Trash)
87 mins

Ripping Yarn: The events portrayed in this film are true. In Pittsburgh in the late 1960s a chemical spill caused the reanimation of dead bodies. George Romero made a film about it called *Night of the Living Dead* but changed the facts to avoid getting sued. In reality, the military were unable to kill the monsters so instead froze the bodies in sealed canisters. Somehow these ended up at Uneeda Medical Supplies. In 1984, Frank and his punk-rocker apprentice Freddie accidentally open one and all hell breaks loose. When a zombie rises, their boss Burt chops the body up and takes it to the mortuary where his buddy Ernie cremates it. The burning corpse releases a noxious gas that, when mixed with rain, spreads the virus all over town. Decomposed cadavers wake and wander the streets looking for something to eat. They're hungry – hungry for 'BRAINNNSSSS!!!!!'

Digging up the Dead: Around the same time as George Romero was shooting *Dawn of the Dead*, his *Night* co-writer John Russo was formulating plans for a sequel of his own. The first movie was a collaboration between the team at Image Ten, so, when it came to a follow-up, it would have been unfair for Romero to claim exclusivity. To differentiate the two potential movie franchises, Russo et al kept the *Living Dead* moniker while Romero's sequels would be labelled *'something' of the Dead*. They agreed this in court.

In 1979 Russo released a novelisation entitled *Return of the Living Dead* that took place two years after the original movie and shared its downbeat tone and countryside location. A movie version directed by Tobe Hooper was in the works but the ongoing court battle with Romero kept it on hold. The project was eventually bought by Tom Fox who axed everything but the title and hired *Alien* screenwriter Dan O'Bannon to direct. He decided to turn the project into a dripping gross-out comedy.

Return of the Living Dead is actually a lot of fun, much more of a popcorn-munching rollercoaster ride than Romero's embittered *Day of the Dead* (which was released the same year). O'Bannon refuses to take his subject matter seriously and his zombies are like walking cartoons; rolling their eyes and lolling their tongues when lusting after juicy brains. These dead things are sprightly too, running around and leaping on ambulance men whenever they get hungry. They even have a halfway decent vocabulary and, after they've eaten a fresh batch of cops, manage to get on the police-car radio receiver to utter, 'Send… more… cops.' It's the undead equivalent of ordering out.

Their attacks are fairly nasty and they greedily scoop out brains from skulls and send geysers of blood across the mortuary floor. The acting matches the absurd feel with larger-than-life performances from the entire cast. James Karen as Frank is jittery and pathetic while the punk kids who crash the town cemetery are typical movie blockheads. They drink beer, smoke cigarettes, read comics and listen to their ghetto blaster at full volume. Later, one of their members, Trash (played by cult scream queen Linnea Quigley), gets turned on when talking about death and strips naked just for the hell of it. She fantasises about being torn apart by old men and later, when the dead walk, gets her wish.

This is comedy at its pitch blackest. The death toll is huge and zombies come back in extreme pain ('I can feel… myself… rotting,' groans one). There is also a sense of hopelessness as whatever the group does to try to stop the ghouls only results in further death. As a rain cloud carries the chemical across America, O'Bannon gleefully seems to be telling us that the end of the world is nigh. But what the hell? You're only dead once, right? Let's party!

Undead or Alive: A ghoulish delight from start to finish. Gore, girls and a great punk soundtrack from the likes of The Cramps and The Damned. What else do you need for a post-pub night in? 4/5

Night of the Living Dead
30th Anniversary Edition (1998)
The horror has been resurrected.

Crew: Director/Writer: John A. Russo, Producer: Russ Streiner, Special Make-Up Effects: Vincent J. Guastini

Cast: Original cast plus, Scott Vladimir Licina (Reverend Hicks), Grant Kramer (Dan), Adam Know (Mike)
93 mins

Ripping Yarn: At the state penitentiary, local idiots Danny and Mike load a coffin into their truck. The body belongs to an executed killer and they drive it to a bleak graveyard somewhere in Pittsburgh. Reverend Hicks and the parents of the girl the dead man killed are waiting. Hicks begins his service. 'We don't believe in cremation,' he rants. 'We believe in the fires of hell. That's the Lord's way of punishing sinners.' The sermon finishes and, as Danny and Mike go about burying the body, it moves. Suddenly the killer gets up and tries to bite Mike. On the opposite side of the cemetery, Johnny and his sister Barbra lay a wreath on their father's grave. In the distance, between the grey headstones, the killer is watching. Night is closing in and tonight it will unleash the living dead...

Digging up the Dead: The 30th anniversary edition of *Night of the Living Dead* is an atrocity – as cynical as it is unskilled – a version of the film to be avoided at all costs. The failure to properly copyright *Night '68* was the cause of much anguish for Image Ten. Almost the minute the film was released it went directly into the public domain, meaning the team behind it made barely a cent. They should have been millionaires. Instead they were living in Pittsburgh.

Over the years they tried numerous tricks to win back copyright but nothing seemed to work. Then came *Star Wars*. In 1997, to mark the 20th anniversary of his space trilogy, George Lucas re-released the entire saga, digitally re-mastered and with deleted scenes reinserted into the movie. It was a sensation, maybe not critically, but certainly in terms of box office. John Russo was making notes. Surely he could do the same and make sure this edition was properly copyrighted.

The original team were gathered – minus George Romero – and went about cutting up the movie, cleaning up the image and adding a new, boring keyboard soundtrack. As far as deleted scenes went (a key factor in the marketing of *Star Wars*), they didn't have any, so an undaunted Russo decided to shoot his own. The new footage, filmed by *The Crazies* cinematographer Bill Hinzman, consisted chiefly of a bizarre wraparound story concerning a disturbed evangelical priest. An epilogue takes place one year later and reveals that Reverend Hicks is immune to zombie bites. All this does is reduce the power of the original.

As Hicks, Scott Vladimir Licina is laughable. His acting is hammy and as he screams about the end of the world – 'Spike the dead to prevent them from rising before Judgement Day!' – and strokes his poodle the film slips into stupidity. He looks out of place too, with his bald head, big white teeth and stylish 1990s goatee. Worst of all is Hinzman, reprising his role as the opening Graveyard Ghoul. All the make-up in the world can't disguise the fact that he's aged 30 years and the new shots jar badly with the original footage of his younger self. With the new revelation that his zombie was a killer in life, his character has now been given a background, which only detracts from the mystery.

The new scenes are a pointless aside to the main action. Nobody cares about this reverend or where that first zombie came from. All we care about is Ben and those people in the farmhouse. The original *Night* is a masterpiece and the disrespect shown here defies belief. Can you imagine anyone doing this to *Citizen Kane*? Romero notoriously hates this version and rumours persist that, on its release, video shops received a record number of returns with people demanding their money back. People felt cheated by this version. This is not *Night of the Living Dead*.

Undead or Alive: Calling the *30th Anniversary Edition* a bastardisation of the original is being generous. The new footage is ugly, modern and without use. Like the zombies that plague the countryside, every copy needs to be rounded up and tossed on a burning pyre. 0/5

28 Days Later (2002)
His fear began when he woke up alone.
His terror began when he realised he wasn't.

Crew: Director: Danny Boyle, Writer: Alex Garland, Producer: Andrew Macdonald, Prosthetic Make-Up Effects: Creature Effects

Cast: Cillian Murphy (Jim), Christopher Eccleston, (Major Henry West), Brendan Gleeson (Frank)
108 mins

Ripping Yarn: In a medical research unit, monkeys are being injected with RAGE, a contagious virus that sends them into a violent mania. One night, environmentalists break in and let one of the monkeys loose…

Twenty-eight days later, Jim wakes up in hospital. The place is empty. He wanders out on to the London streets looking for someone – anyone. The sun sets against Big Ben. Jim is alone. Nearby, he discovers a church awash with bodies. An insane priest attacks him and the others wake up and charge after him. Jim is rescued by Mark and Selena, two survivors living in the ashes of old London. RAGE has infected the population. Later, Mark is killed and Jim and Selena find a middle-aged cabbie called Frank surviving in the city with his daughter Hannah. Together they aim to travel to a military compound near Manchester. But there they might just find something worse than infection…

Digging up the Dead: 'To those people who say *28 Days Later* is a rip-off of George Romero I would say… if you're gonna borrow, you borrow from the best.'[3] Director Danny Boyle's comments were said with a knowing wink, but there's no disguising the fact that his movie barely contains a single original idea. He picks Romero's back catalogue clean. When stopping for fuel, Jim checks out a nearby food cabin and is forced to kill an infected child. This happens to Peter in 1978's *Dawn*. A chained-up infected soldier is clearly Bub from *Day* and there's even a shopping sequence where the group pick up luxuries like chocolate, coffee and whiskey from an abandoned supermarket. 'Let's shop,' says Selena. Anyone who's seen *Dawn* doesn't need telling where this comes from.

The film borrows key concepts (and sometimes whole scenes) from Romero but its chief source of 'inspiration' is somewhat closer to home. John Wyndham's classic 1951 British novel *Day of the Triffids* begins in an empty hospital. Protagonist Bill Masen wakes up and wanders on to the deserted London streets. Amidst a global catastrophe he falls in with a female survivor and together they abandon the capital in favour of the countryside. Along the way they find a young girl alone and create a surrogate family. Eventually they encounter a corrupt military organisation led by a redheaded man. Meanwhile, the killer plants known as triffids take over England. Replace triffids with the Infected and this is the plot of Danny Boyle's movie exactly. Christopher Eccleston's Major West even has red hair!

Swapping zombies/triffids for infected people is a neat idea (even though Romero already did this in *The Crazies*) but Boyle is never clear as to the exact nature of the virus. Early on, an expository lab assistant tells us it sends the carrier into an uncontrollable fury. But, if this is the case, why don't the Infected attack each other? Also, when they've got their victims, they're not particularly violent, merely puking contagious blood on to whomever they're flailing at. You expect something so violent to kill its subject, but, since there are so many Infected, this is clearly not the case. There's a lot here that doesn't make sense.

Where *28 Days* is more successful is in the visual realisation of the movie. Boyle is the renowned director of Brit-pop classic *Trainspotting* (1996) and he clearly has a flair for exciting storytelling. The use of DV cameras and disjointed editing gives *28 Days* a raw, unstoppable edge that reflects the schizophrenic nature of the Infected. As Jim races away from the diseased masses in the church, we see flames flick in front of the camera. These flames belong to a firebomb. As the Infected are set on fire, the camera speeds up and slows down and moves about with a maddening wrath that flings us unwittingly into the action. There is an originality here that is missing from every other aspect of the movie.

Undead or Alive: On its release the film caught the public's imagination and began a renewed interest in zombie cinema. With hindsight, however, Boyle was right. This is nothing more than a well-crafted rip-off. 2/5

Shaun of the Dead (2004)
A romantic comedy. With zombies.

Crew: Director: Edgar Wright, Producer: Nira Park, Writers: Simon Pegg & Edgar Wright, Special Effects: Special Effects UK

Cast: Simon Pegg (Shaun), Kate Ashfield (Liz), Nick Frost (Ed) 95 mins

Ripping Yarn: Shaun needs to grow up. He's 29 and spends most of his time hanging out with his best friend Ed and drinking beer at the Winchester. His girlfriend Liz wants something more and her friends Dianne and David ('a failed actress and a twat') think she deserves better. Shaun promises to take her out to dinner but, when he forgets, Liz dumps him. He is mortified and, that night, drowns his sorrows down the local. The next day the dead begin to rise and start eating people. Realising that they're on the brink of global catastrophe, Shaun calls his mum. She's okay but his stepdad Phillip has been bitten so Shaun hatches a plan: 'Go to Mum's, kill Phil, grab Liz, go to the Winchester, have a nice cold pint and wait for all this to blow over.' It should work out fine – just don't mention the 'Z word'.

Digging up the Dead: 'We're coming to get you, Barbara,' hollers Ed down the phone to Shaun's mum, and, from the minute the dead walk, Edgar Wright invites us into a loving and full-blooded tribute to Romero's *Dead* saga. Gone are the running and jumping zombies of *28 Days Later*, these are dead creatures in the George A. Romero fashion: wobbling, twisted and 'all messed up'. *Shaun* is a comedy, but one that treats its subject matter with respect.

These are ferocious creatures hungry for flesh and the humour comes not from them (as it did in *Return of the Living Dead*) but from the characters and their reactions. 'She's so drunk,' observes Shaun on first seeing a zombie stumble into frame. When he discovers she's actually a walking corpse, he reacts by throwing old records at her head – but only the ones he doesn't want anymore. 'The *Batman* soundtrack?' asks Ed. 'Throw it!' cries Shaun. Later, when a Groom Zombie gets into his house, Shaun gives an appropriately adolescent screech: 'Ooh, he's got an arm off!'

To keep Romero fans happy, the film is full of sly references to the man's movies. There's Foree Electrics, the company Shaun works for, and there's also his pretty spot-on impersonation of *Day*'s Bub when the group pretend to be zombies. This said, *Shaun of the Dead* is far more than just fanboy homage and expertly fuses knockabout humour (such as the continual pounding of a zombie's skull in time with Queen's 'Don't Stop me Now') with moments of genuine emotion. Shaun's relationship with Liz is tender and Kate Ashfield is so sweet natured that it's easy to see why Shaun would risk everything to save her. For his part, Simon Pegg reveals himself to be a skilled actor and when he finds out his mum has been bitten he is genuinely affecting and grounds the film in a tragic reality. Pegg has the makings of a very strong, very likeable leading man.

Where the film also scores points is in its Britishness. There are obvious gags about drinking tea but more intriguing are the suggestions of how the English would react in such a crisis. The country's 'mind your own business' approach to life means Shaun is slow to realise what's going on. He walks to the shops with his head down, passing smashed cars, stumbling over dead people and a fridge smeared with bloody handprints. Only when a dead person shows up in his own back garden does he spring into action, wielding the most effectively English weapon he can find – a cricket bat.

Wright's direction is knowing and energetic (the brilliant crash-zoom montages of Ed making tea or using the toilet are wonderful spoofs of 'tooling-up' sequences in films like *Evil Dead 2*) and the script is frequently laugh-out-loud funny. The film only falters at the end, when the British Army show up and save the day. In Romero movies, the military are never the good guys.

Undead or Alive: Not only one of the best zombie spoofs ever made, but also perhaps one of the finest British comedies full stop. Romero loved it. 5/5

No More Room in Hell

Perhaps because of his independence and the difficulty in financing movies outside of Hollywood, Romero has had more unmade projects than almost anyone in cinema history. Even his idol Orson Welles, who had a slew of half-finished films at the time of his death, can't boast as many disappointments as Romero. But not all of these were to be low-budget productions and some were the result of a brief fling with Hollywood. Studio executives, imagining they were making hip films with a genuine maverick, would later turn around and play it safe at the last minute. There are some interesting ideas here and many of them would have made wonderful movies. In time, maybe some of them still will.

The Assassination – A film about the real-life Dominican dictator Rafael Trujillo who held his country in a stranglehold from 1930 to 1961. He was eventually disposed of by revolutionary assassins supported by the CIA. Anthony Quinn was set to star as Trujillo alongside singer Ricky Martin and Ed Harris. Quinn's sad death caused the project to be cancelled.

Aurora, Texas – A UFO story.

Before I Wake – A ghost story for MGM that dominated five years of Romero's life and was partially responsible for his time in the wilderness from 1993 to 2000. Around $1 million was spent on offices, numerous drafts, designs and finding locations. When MGM finally passed, the script went to 20th Century Fox, but when the budget exceeded $20 million the project became cast dependent. When Meryl Streep, Gwyneth Paltrow and Sharon Stone all declined, the movie was shelved.

Black Mariah – In 1993 New Line Cinema acquired the rights to a novel called *The Black Mariah*. Romero wrote a script but the film never found its way into production.

The Calling – Romero wrote a screenplay on spec.

Carnivore – Written by *The Matrix* (1999) directors the Wachowski Brothers who would also have co-produced.

Diamond Dead – A horror-comedy-musical about a resurrected heavy-metal band. David Bowie, Johnny Depp, Marilyn Manson (in the role of Jesus Christ), Ozzy Osbourne, Asia Argento, Gwen Stefani and Ian McKellen were all considered for parts. Songs were written by *The Rocky Horror Picture Show's* (1975) Richard Hartley and Ridley and Tony Scott were onboard as producers. The project fell through when Romero left to helm *Land of the Dead*.

Dracula – TV miniseries for ABC in 2004 based on the story by Bram Stoker. The studio eventually chose to green light Stephen King's *Kingdom Hospital* instead.

Firestarter – A Stephen King adaptation about a girl with telekinetic powers. Romero was approached to direct but the job eventually went to Mark L. Lester in 1984. The film starred a young Drew Barrymore.

Flying Horses – A man who lives on an island. Denzel Washington was first choice to star.

Frankenstein – In 1982 Romero wrote a rough draft of a script for television based on Mary Shelley's classic novel.

From a Buick 8 – Adaptation of the Stephen King novel about a car that acts as a gateway to other evil dimensions. The project was taken over in 2007 by Tobe Hooper.

The Girl Who Loved Tom Gordon – Romero wrote a screenplay based on the book by Stephen King about a girl who gets lost in the woods. Dakota Fanning was going to play 'The Girl', with Laura Dern as her mother. The script was written in 2001. Romero almost got it into production after *Land of the Dead*.

Goosebumps – Based on the children's horror stories by R.L. Stine. A TV series ran from 1995 to 1998. Viewer Beware! You're in for a scare!

Gunperson – 1973 treatment for an all-female western.

The Ill – A story about a college boy's love for a girl who spreads a virus that turns people into vampires. Would have starred Asia Argento.

Land of the Dead 2 – Would have been the first *Dead* sequel to use the characters from the preceding movie. Shelved after *Land*'s poor performance at the box office.

Masters of Horror – Horror television series with each episode directed by a different master of the genre. The show was first broadcast in 2005 with contributions from John Landis, John Carpenter, Dario Argento, Joe Dante and Takashi Miike. Romero agreed to take part but later pulled out.

Mongrel: The Legend of Copperhead – A self-penned superhero written by Romero in conjunction with Marvel Comics (creators of *Spider-Man*). Mongrel is the sheriff of Philadelphia in the not-too-distant future. Tie-in merchandise and comic books were planned.

Moonshadows – A horror film for children.

The Mummy – A direct horror remake of the 1932 original starring Boris Karloff. The project was green lit with a $12 million budget but Romero was unable to get away from his duties on *Before I Wake*. Bore little resemblance to the 1999 version directed by Stephen Sommers.

Night of the Living Dead TV Series – In 1998, Granada TV wanted to make a television series in the UK.

Quevira – Amy Madigan and Ed Harris wanted to work with Romero on this film.

Red Eye: Flight of the Living Dead – Bore no resemblance to either Wes Craven's *Red Eye* (2005) or 2007's *Flight of the Living Dead*.

Resident Evil – After directing a trailer for Capcom's *Resident Evil 2* computer game, Romero was approached to direct a feature adaptation. His script was faithful to the first game but was rejected because of its extreme gore and adult nature. Paul Anderson directed a teen-friendly version in 2002.

Scream – Before Wes Craven, Romero was offered the chance to direct 1997's post–modern slasher flick. He turned it down.

Salem's Lot – Based on Stephen King's novel about vampires in a small town. Before Romero, numerous people attempted an adaptation, including Mike Nichols and Larry Cohen. Romero pulled out when executives at Warner Brothers decided to make it as a TV miniseries. The television adaptation was screened in 1979 and directed by Tobe Hooper.

Shoo-be Doo-be Moon – Homage to 1950s science fiction written by *There's Always Vanilla* scribe Rudolph Ricci. The film was to be the third picture in a deal with UFD following *Knightriders* and *Creepshow*. May have been partly based on an earlier Ricci screenplay entitled *Invasion of the Spaghetti Monsters*.

Solitary Isle – An expedition to a deserted island takes a deadly turn when the explorers encounter a malevolent unknown force. Based on the story by *Ringu* writer Koji Suzuki.

The Stand – Another proposed Stephen King adaptation. The book dealt with an apocalyptic plague and ran at nearly 600 pages. Laurel producer Richard Rubinstein called it 'epic – in the David Lean sense of the word'.[1] Romero planned to release it as two movies, *The Stand* and *The Plague*. In 1994, Mick Garris directed a TV version for Laurel.

Tarzan – Based on the stories by Edgar Rice Burroughs. It's Romero's dream project and he has wanted to direct a version all his life.

The Turn of the Screw – Adaptation of the Henry James novel about a governess looking after two children who may or may not be possessed. Romero wrote a screenplay with Michael Hirst for Columbia Pictures. The story had been filmed before in 1961 as *The Innocents* directed by Jack Clayton.

Unholy Fire – An adaptation of the novel by *Communion* writer Whitley Strieber. The story told of a woman found brutally murdered in a New York church and the police's attempts to find the killer. Strieber wrote the screenplay himself and hoped Romero would begin directing in 1993. He never did.

War of the Worlds – Based on the novel by H.G. Wells. Later made into a TV series and then a film directed by Steven Spielberg in 2005.

Whine of the Fawn – A story about two medieval teenagers.

X-Files episode – Was to be written by Stephen King and made to commemorate *Night of the Living Dead*. Mulder and Scully would presumably have had to take on some zombies. The episode fell through when Stephen King became too busy to contribute.

References

Introduction: American Maverick

1 Romero quoted in *Hall of Fame: George Romero*, Horror Mark, 2007 (Available on www.horrormark.com)

2 Romero quoted on *Real Horrorwood*, Real Audio, 1998 (No longer available)

3 Lyon, Christopher & Doll, Susan (Eds), *International Dictionary of Films and Filmmakers,* Pan Macmillan, 1987, p.712

Blue Collar Monsters

1 Brown, Tom, *Night of the Living Dead: 25th Anniversary Documentary,* The Suburban Temp Company, 1993 (Available on Anchor Bay Entertainment Region 2 DVD)

2 Beaupre, Lee, 'Review of *Night of the Living Dead*', *Variety*, 16 October 1968, p.6

3 Hertz, Gary, *Digging up the Dead: The 'Lost' Films of George A. Romero,* Anchor Bay, 2005 (Available on Anchor Bay Entertainment Region 1 DVD)

4 Pirie, David, 'Review of *Jack's Wife*', *Time Out 625*, 20 April 1982, p.23

5 Romero, George, *The Crazies Audio Commentary,* Anchor Bay, 2003 (Available on Anchor Bay Entertainment Region 2 DVD)

6 Romero quoted in *The Living Dead 2000,* www.winny.com, 2003 (No longer available)

Weird Fantasies and Tales of Fear

1 Kroll, Jack, 'Review of *Martin*', *Newsweek,* July 1978

2 Chute, David, 'Tom Savini: Maniac', *Film Comment 17/4,* July–August 1981, p.24

3 Romero, George & Sparrow, Susanna, *Martin Novelisation: Afterword,* Glasgow: Futura Publications Limited, 1978, p.213

4 Unknown, *Making Martin: A Recounting,* Lions Gate Entertainment, 2004 (Available on Arrow Films Region 2 DVD)

5 Gagne, Paul R., *The Zombies That Ate Pittsburgh,* New York: Dodd, Mead and Co, 1987, p.83

6 Ebert, Roger, 'Review of *Dawn of the Dead*', *Chicago Sun Times,* 4 May 1979

7 Brown, Paul J. with Burrell, Nigel J., *Savini: The Wizard of Gore,* Cambridge: Midnight Media, 1997, p.20

8 Skal, David J, *The Monster Show: A Cultural History of Horror,* London: Plexus, 1993, p.311

9 Yakir, Dan, 'Knight after Night with George Romero', *American Film 6/7*, May 1981, p.45

10 Palopoli, Steve, 'George Romero: Don of the Dead', *Total Movie*, 1 February 2001, p.78

11 Reed, Rex, 'Review of *Creepshow*', *New York Post*, November 1982

12 Gagne, Paul R., *The Zombies That Ate Pittsburgh*, New York: Dodd, Mead and Co, 1987, p.124

13 Wood, Robin, *Hollywood: From Vietnam to Reagan*, New York: Columbia University Press, 1986, p.191

14 Harmetz, Aljean, 'From the Cecil B. DeMilles of Pittsburgh: "Creepshow"', *New York Times*, 7 November 1982, p.16

15 Martin, Perry, *The Many Days of Day of the Dead,* Anchor Bay, 2005 (Available on Anchor Bay Entertainment Region 1 DVD)

16 Levi, Dean, 'Review of *Day of the Dead*', *Richmond, Virginia News Leader*, 1985

17 Ronald Reagan quoted on Washburn, J., *Not too Late for a War Crimes Tribunal*, Vander Hashish, 2001 (Available on: www.vanderhashish.com)

Hollywood Horror Show

1 Kermode, Mark, 'Twilight's Last Gleaming – George A. Romero', *Monthly Film Bulletin 57/673*, February 1990, p.40

2 Szebin, Frederick C., 'George Romero's *Ella*', *Cinefantastique 18/5*, July1988, p.17

3 Frasher, Michael, '*Night of the Living Dead*: Remaking George Romero's Horror Classic', *Cinefantastique 21/3*, December 1990, p.17

4 Author's interview, 2008

5 Brown, Paul J. with Burrell, Nigel J., *Savini: The Wizard of Gore*, Cambridge: Midnight Media, 1997, p.45

6 Palopoli, Steve, 'George Romero: Don of the Dead', *Total Movie*, 1 February 2001, p.78

7 Leayman, Charles, 'Filming Stephen King's Horror *The Dark Half*, *Cinefantastique 24/1*, June 1993, p.19

Back from the Dead

1 Hart, Hugh, 'Dead Man Talking', *San Francisco Chronicle*, 26 July 2005, p.PK-24

2 Rowe, Michael, 'Face to No Face with Bruiser', *Fangoria 211*, April 2001, p.76

3 Porton, Richard, 'Blue Collar Monsters: An Interview with George Romero', *Filmhäftet 119*, 2002, p.1

4 Dinning, Mark, 'Rom' Comms', *Total Film 107*, October 2005, p.120

5 Epstein, Daniel Robert, 'Land of the Dead: An Interview

with George Romero', *Underground Online*, 2005, available on www.ugo.com

6 George W. Bush quoted at the Al Smith Diner in New York, 2000

7 Interview with George Romero on *Diary of the Dead*, Cinema Blend, 2007 (Available on www.cinemablend.com)

8 Kay, Jeremy, 'Rebirth of the Dead', *Screen International 1564*, 22 September 2006, p.8

9 Alexander, Chris, 'Diary of the Dead: First-Person Ghouling', *Fangoria 270*, February 2008, p.48

10 Clark, Sean, Interview with George A. Romero, 2007 (Available on www.youtube.com)

Children of the Living Dead

1 Russell, Jamie, *Book of the Dead: The Complete History of Zombie Cinema*, Surrey: FAB Press, 2005, p.142

2 Nails, Rusty, *Dead On: The Life and Cinema of George A. Romero*, New Eye Films, 2008 (Currently unavailable)

No More Room in Hell

1 Jones, Stephen, *Creepshows: The Illustrated Stephen King Movie Guide*, London: Titan Books, 2001, p.87

Bibliography

Gagne, Paul R., *The Zombies That Ate Pittsburgh: The Films of George A. Romero*, New York: Dodd, Mead & Co, 1987

Jones, Stephen, *Creepshows: The Illustrated Stephen King Movie Guide*, London: Titan Books, 2001

King, Stephen, *The Dark Half*, London: Hodder & Stoughton, 1989

Paffenroth, Kim, *The Gospel of the Living Dead: George Romero's Visions of Hell on Earth*, Texas: Baylor University Press, 2006

Russell, Jamie, *Book of the Dead: The Complete History of Zombie Cinema*, Surrey: FAB Press, 2005

Russo, John, *Return of the Living Dead*, London: Hamlyn, 1979

Skal, David J., *The Monster Show: A Cultural History of Horror*, London: Plexus, 1994

Stewart, Michael, *Monkey Shines*, London: Macmillan, 1983

Williams, Tony, *The Cinema of George A. Romero: Knight of the Living Dead*, London: Wallflower Press, 2003

Websites

www.homepageofthedead.com – Valuable resource on
  Romero's *Dead* saga

www.savini.com – Official homepage of the wizard of gore

www.kenforee.co.uk – Your UK guide to Ken Foree and
  Foree Fest

Index